SpringerBriefs in Computer Science

SpringerBriefs present concise summaries of cutting-edge research and practical applications across a wide spectrum of fields. Featuring compact volumes of 50 to 125 pages, the series covers a range of content from professional to academic.

Typical topics might include:

- A timely report of state-of-the art analytical techniques
- A bridge between new research results, as published in journal articles, and a contextual literature review
- A snapshot of a hot or emerging topic
- An in-depth case study or clinical example
- A presentation of core concepts that students must understand in order to make independent contributions

Briefs allow authors to present their ideas and readers to absorb them with minimal time investment. Briefs will be published as part of Springer's eBook collection, with millions of users worldwide. In addition, Briefs will be available for individual print and electronic purchase. Briefs are characterized by fast, global electronic dissemination, standard publishing contracts, easy-to-use manuscript preparation and formatting guidelines, and expedited production schedules. We aim for publication 8–12 weeks after acceptance. Both solicited and unsolicited manuscripts are considered for publication in this series.

**Indexing: This series is indexed in Scopus, Ei-Compendex, and zbMATH **

Guoming Tang • Deke Guo • Kui Wu

GreenEdge: New Perspectives to Energy Management and Supply in Mobile Edge Computing

The First Book on Green Edge Computing

Springer

Guoming Tang 🆔
Department of Broadband Communication
Peng Cheng Laboratory
Shenzhen, China

Deke Guo
College of Systems Engineering
National University of Defense Technology
Changsha, Hunan, China

Kui Wu
Department of Computer Science
University of Victoria
Victoria, BC, Canada

ISSN 2191-5768   ISSN 2191-5776 (electronic)
SpringerBriefs in Computer Science
ISBN 978-981-16-9689-3   ISBN 978-981-16-9690-9 (eBook)
https://doi.org/10.1007/978-981-16-9690-9

This Springer imprint is published by the registered company Springer Nature Singapore Pte Ltd.
The registered company address is: 152 Beach Road, #21-01/04 Gateway East, Singapore 189721, Singapore

Preface

The 5G technology has been commercialized worldwide and is expected to provide superior performance with enhanced mobile broadband, ultra-low latency transmission, and massive IoT connections. Meanwhile, the edge computing paradigm gets popular to provide distributed computing and storage resources in proximity to the users (at the network edge). Compared with cloud computing, edge computing has the advantage of conducting latency-critical tasks by having them executed closer to end users. As edge services and applications prosper, 5G and edge computing will be tightly coupled and continuously promote each other forward. Embracing this trend, however, mobile users, infrastructure providers, and service providers are all faced with the energy dilemma. From the user side, battery-powered mobile devices are much constrained by battery life, whereas mobile platforms and apps nowadays are usually power-hungry. From the infrastructure and service provider side, the energy cost of edge facilities, particularly 5G base stations and edge datacenters, accounts for a large proportion of operating expenses and has become a huge burden.

In this book, we introduce our recent work tackling the energy issues in mobile edge computing. We name the constellation of work **GreenEdge**. Unlike traditional approaches, solutions, and frameworks, we deal with energy management and supply problems from totally new perspectives. For mobile users, (i) we investigate their low-battery anxiety through a large-scale user survey and quantify their anxiety degree and video watching behavior concerning the battery status; and (ii) by leveraging the quantified low-battery anxiety model, we further develop a low-power video streaming solution at the network edge to save mobile devices' energy and alleviate users' low-battery anxiety. For edge infrastructure and service operators, (i) we devise an optimal backup power deployment framework to cut down the backup battery cost in 5G networks; (ii) we investigate the cost-saving potential of transforming the backup batteries to a distributed battery energy storage system; and (iii) we design an integrated renewable energy supply architecture and a software-defined power supply mechanism to pursue net-zero edge datacenters in the future edge computing environment.

Shenzhen, China   Guoming Tang
Changsha, China   Deke Guo
Victoria, BC, Canada   Kui Wu

Contents

Chapter 1
Introduction

1.1 When 5G Meets Edge Computing

The twenty-first century has witnessed tremendous progress in computing and communication. On the one hand, with the development of wireless communications, the fifth-generation mobile network (5G network) has been commercialized since 2019. Compared with 4G/LTE, 5G shows superior performance with enhanced mobile broadband, ultra-low latency transmission, and massive Internet of Things (IoT) connections. On the other hand, as an important complement to cloud computing, the edge computing paradigm emerges and aims to provide distributed computing resources in the form of edge servers for services at the network edge. Having tasks performed closer to the users, edge computing leads to a shorter delay and higher quality of service (QoS) and quality of experience (QoE).

With advanced communication performance, more data can be uploaded to the cloud and delivered through the Internet. Meanwhile, aided by the powerful computing capacity of edge servers, large service requests can be satisfied promptly at the network edge, without the need of passing through the backbone networks to the cloud. As edge services prosper, 5G and edge computing will be tightly coupled and continuously promote each other forward.

As major customers of 5G and edge services, mobile users nowadays are increasingly dependent on mobile phones for daily communication, study, and business. In 2020, the population of worldwide mobile users had exceeded 3.5 billion and was expected to grow in the future [1]. Thus, it is of significant importance to understand mobile users' behaviours in terms of reactions and interactions when using mobile phones. The corresponding findings and insights could provide helpful guidance to mobile users for proper and healthy mobile usage. They also have significant business values for the mobile OS or app designer (e.g., in improving user interfaces) and mobile service provider (e.g., in enhancing QoS/QoE).

© The Author(s), under exclusive license to Springer Nature Singapore Pte Ltd. 2022
G. Tang et al., *GreenEdge: New Perspectives to Energy Management and Supply in Mobile Edge Computing*, SpringerBriefs in Computer Science, https://doi.org/10.1007/978-981-16-9690-9_1

In support of 5G and edge computing, a large number of edge facilities have been constructed and deployed by the infrastructure and service providers, including access points, base stations, edge nodes/servers, and micro/mini datacenters [2]. Base stations (BSs) are the key facilities in 5G networks and have been built in large quantities worldwide these years. According to [3], China will build over 14 million 5G BSs by 2026. Compared with the older generation networks like 4G/LTE, the signal range of a 5G base station is much shorter, resulting in ultra-dense BS deployment, especially for full signal coverage in urban or "hotspot" areas. In addition, service providers are deploying their own datacenters (DCs) located close to the customers they serve, known as "edge DCs". Like the traditional cloud DCs, the edge DCs deliver computing resources and cached contents to end users, whereas their sizes/scales are normally much smaller than the cloud. The geo-distributed small-size edge DCs are expected to serve particular customer groups near them and act as key enablers of the diverse edge services in future.

1.2 The Energy Dilemma

In the era of 5G and edge computing, mobile users, infrastructure providers, and service providers are all faced with the energy dilemma.

For Mobile Users

As battery-powered devices, the constrained battery life of mobile phones may greatly limit their ubiquitous usages in the daily life of mobile users. Nevertheless, mobile platforms and apps nowadays are usually power-hungry, making battery power more precious than ever. By looking into the power consumption of different mobile phones in video streaming applications, we have found that the mobile battery power drains quickly, and the display module is the primary energy guzzler [4]. Consequently, low battery in mobile phones can bring wide impacts on users' behaviours and emotions. Evidence has shown that over 20% of the mobile audiences will stop watching videos when the battery life remains 20%, and the percentage quickly rises to 50% when only 10% battery energy is left [5].

For Infrastructure and Service Operators

While 5G has a significant performance improvement over 4G, the shifting from 4G to 5G needs enormous investments from the infrastructure operators, covering both capital expense (CAPEX) and operating expense (OPEX). The OPEX, in particular, is mainly attributed to the electricity consumed by the base stations. According to the power measurements from the mobile operators, the power consumption of a 5G base station is typically 2~3 times that of a 4G base station. Considering the ultra-dense deployment of base stations in 5G/B5G networks, it could lead up to a tenfold increase in electricity cost [6]. Meanwhile, the ever-increasing demands for computation and storage by various edge services drive the edge servers scaling out and up rapidly, incurring enormous energy consumption at geo-distributed edge DCs. It has been reported that the energy cost accounts for more than half of the

OPEX in datacenters nowadays. Consequently, the energy cost has become a heavy burden to the infrastructure and service operators.

1.3 Key Problems and Contributions

Quantifying Low-Battery Anxiety and Its Impacts
The heavy dependence on the mobile phone has incurred a new phenomenon of low-battery anxiety (LBA) among modern mobile users [7]. Although being unveiled for a while, LBA has not been thoroughly investigated yet. Without a better understanding of LBA, it would be difficult to precisely validate energy saving and management techniques in terms of alleviating LBA and enhancing QoE. To fill the gap, we conduct an investigation over 2000+ mobile users, look into their feelings and reactions towards LBA, and quantify their anxiety degree during the draining of battery power. As a case study, we also investigate the impact of LBA on user's behaviour at video watching, and with the massive answers we are able to quantify user's likelihood of abandoning attractive videos versus the battery status of mobile phones. The findings and quantitative models not only disclose the characteristics of LBA among modern mobile users, but also provide valuable references for the design, evaluation, and improvement of QoE-aware mobile services.

User Energy and LBA Aware Mobile Video Streaming
The LBA of mobile users could cause customer loss, especially in power-hungry mobile services like video streaming [5]. By leveraging the quantitative model obtained from the large-scale user survey, we design tailored mechanisms for energy-saving and LBA alleviation in mobile video streaming. Specifically, by exploiting the emerging edge computing paradigm, we propose a novel solution for low-power video streaming (LPVS) at the network edge. It aims to minimize the LBA of mobile users by integrating the LBA model with the low-power video transforming techniques. To accommodate the heterogeneous LBA properties of mobile users under different circumstances, we also develop an LBA model updating scheme by further considering the specific and local edge environments. The emulation results using real-world video watching traces demonstrate that LPVS can effectively alleviate mobile users' LBA and prolong their video-watching time (i.e., customer retention) by 39%.

Optimal Management of BS Backup Power for 5G Networks
The shift of mobile networks from 4G/LTE to 5G will lead to an explosive growth of 5G base stations. To guarantee the network reliability for 5G-enabled services, however, an extremely large number of backup batteries would be needed for the densely deployed base stations. To cut the battery cost while ensuring network reliability, we propose ShiftGuard, an optimal backup power deployment framework. By leveraging the power demand differences among base stations from both spatial and temporal dimensions, ShiftGuard gives the most cost-efficient backup power allocation solution under the constraints of network reliability and

real-world deployment factors. Experimental results demonstrate that compared to the strategy without backup power sharing or simply sharing with nearby BSs, ShiftGuard can cut the battery cost by 27∼40%.

In operating 5G networks, the high energy consumption of base stations is one major concern, and how to reduce the energy cost is among the top priorities. To this end, we investigate the energy cost-saving potential by transforming the backup batteries of base stations to a distributed battery energy storage system (BESS). Specifically, to minimize the total energy cost, we model the distributed BESS discharge/charge scheduling as an optimization problem by incorporating comprehensive practical considerations. Then, considering the dynamic BS power demands in practice, we develop a deep reinforcement learning (DRL) based approach to make BESS scheduling decisions in real-time. The experiments using real-world BS deployment and traffic load data demonstrate that, with our DRL-based BESS scheduling, the peak power demand charge of BSs can be reduced by up to 26.59%, and the yearly OPEX saving for 2282 5G BSs could reach up to US$185,000.

Software-Defined Power Supply to Geo-Distributed Edge DCs
Due to the dramatic growth of energy consumption and the corresponding carbon footprints at edge DCs, it is an interesting yet challenging problem to maximize the utilization of onsite renewable energy and achieve net-zero edge DCs. To this end, we propose a software-defined power supply (SDPS) architecture to maximize the utilization of renewable energy in supplying the geo-distributed edge DCs. The SDPS architecture adopts i) "green cell" integration and ii) BESS with two-phase power supply operations. Specifically, we formulate the two phases as two mixed integer programming problems, respectively, and minimize the brown power consumption in supplying the edge DCs. Experiments with real-world trace data show that SDPS achieves superior performances than the conventional power supply architectures in improving the renewable energy utilization across the edge DCs.

1.4   Content Organization

The rest of this book is organized as follows.

In Chap. 2, we investigate the low-battery anxiety among modern mobile users by conducting a large-scale user survey. Specifically, we quantify the anxiety degree of mobile users and their likelihood of abandoning video watching with respect to the battery status, respectively.

In Chap. 3, we develop a novel solution to low-power video streaming service at the network edge for mobile energy saving and LBA alleviating, leveraging the quantified LBA model in Chap. 2.

In Chap. 4, we devise an optimal backup power deployment framework to reduce the backup battery cost in 5G networks.

In Chap. 5, we investigate the cost-saving potential of transforming the backup batteries to a distributed BESS in mobile networks.

In Chap. 6, we propose a software-defined power supply architecture and two-phase BESS aided power supply regulations for net-zero edge DCs in the future edge computing environment.

In Chap. 7, we conclude the book and propose potential research problems for future work.

Chapter 2
Investigating Low-Battery Anxiety of Mobile Users

2.1 Introduction

"Have you ever ordered something at a bar just so you can ask to plug in your phone? Do you argue with loved ones because your phone died and you missed their calls or texts? Are you regularly accused of secretly 'borrowing' someone else's charger? If so, you may be suffering from 'Low-Battery Anxiety' ", according to a survey conducted by LG [7]. The survey also reported a shocking result—nine out of ten mobile users have the so-called low-battery anxiety (LBA), which refers to one's fear of losing mobile phone battery power especially when it is already at a low level (20% for example). The fear of losing battery power further triggers the "no-mobile-phone phobia" (nomophobia), which is commonly considered as one social phobia and could lead to mental health problems [8]. Considering the ever increasing number of smartphone users worldwide, the impact of accompanying LBA could be profound.

To accommodate the dying battery, people tend to change their behavior. For instance, the LG survey found that one in three people are likely to skip the gym, when it comes to choosing between hitting the gym and charging their smartphones. Those who severely suffer from the LBA were reported to behave strangely, e.g., head home immediately, ask chargers from strangers, secretly "borrow" other's charger, or stop answering friends' calls [7]. Also, the ubiquitous LBA is said to potentially harm our social relationships. Sixty percent of the LG surveyed mobile users blamed a dead phone for not speaking to their family members, friends or colleagues if their battery was low.

Understanding users' behavior when facing low battery level has a significant business meaning. In recent years, video streaming services at the mobile end are booming, triggered by the ubiquitous usage of mobile devices and emerging techniques in networking/computing [9]. The already-popular over-the-top (OTT) video delivery as well as the new-generation HD, 4K or 8K video contents are

G. Tang et al., *GreenEdge: New Perspectives to Energy Management and Supply in Mobile Edge Computing*, SpringerBriefs in Computer Science, https://doi.org/10.1007/978-981-16-9690-9_2

making the mobile video streaming service one of the key features in the near 5G era. This new trend has fostered several fast-growing companies in mobile video-sharing services, such as Instagram and ByteDance. The view counts and the time of video watching directly impact the companies' revenue and customer retention rate. We have found that during the mobile video streaming, people tend to value between the attractiveness of a video and their battery power. This is mainly because playing video could consume a large portion of the total power of a mobile phone. According to our findings from a large-scale user survey, mobile users may leave an attractive video at high probability when the battery power is low (Sect. 2.5). Therefore, for mobile video streaming service providers, LBA directly impacts the customer retention rate and should be regarded as an important quality of experience (QoE) metric.

A great deal of research has been devoted to saving energy and prolonging the battery lifetime of mobile phones. For example, tremendous efforts have been made to save energy of the major components of mobile phones, including CPU [10], communication [11], and display [12]. Particularly in pervasive and ubiquitous computing, energy efficient techniques have been developed for mobile sensing/crowdsensing [13], wireless communication [14], and battery management [15]. Nevertheless, from the viewpoint of alleviating the LBA of mobile users, how effective were these energy saving approaches and how could we further improve them? These questions have remained largely unanswered. One of the biggest challenges to answer the above questions is the lack of a quantitative study of mobile users' LBA. As the anxiety of mobile users refers to a subjective feeling or emotion of human beings, it is hard to precisely quantify with some existing metric.

Generally speaking, "if you cannot measure it, you cannot manage it." Due to the lack of LBA quantification, we can neither precisely measure the severity of anxiety among modern mobile users, nor accurately evaluate the effects of mobile energy saving strategies on LBA relief. A better understanding of mobile users' psychology and behavior leads to more effective and even new solutions to the LBA problem. This directly motivates our work in this chapter: *quantifying mobile users' LBA and as a case study investigating its impact on the mobile video streaming service.*

Among existing pervasive computing research, however, very few work on LBA quantification can be found. Although there are relevant literature on the human-battery interaction (HBI) [16–19], they are usually subject to two pitfalls: i) the analysis was performed in a qualitative way over the mobile users [7, 19], and thus the conclusions cannot be leveraged for quantitative evaluations; ii) the investigation was made for a specific and small user group [16–18], and thus the obtained findings have limited generalizability for a large population. In this work, we not only conduct a large-scale investigation about the LBA issue, but also build LBA related quantitative models. Specifically, we set to answer three research questions

- (**RQ1**) How severe is the LBA among modern mobile users?
- (**RQ2**) How can we quantify the LBA and extract quantitative models from the survey of a large-group of mobile users?

- **(RQ3)** How can we quantify the impacts of LBA on mobile users' video watching behavior, e.g., giving up watching an attractive video?

By answering the above questions, we make the following contributions in this work.

- We conduct a user survey over 2000+ mobile users and present a comprehensive study that addresses various aspects of the LBA issue. This leads to many interesting and insightful findings based on analysis of different user groups.
- We present the methodology to extract the LBA curve through the surveyed data and obtain quantified anxiety degrees of the mobile users over varying battery levels. This provides a quantitative model for the mobile energy management research, especially the analysis and optimization of QoE-aware mobile applications/services.
- We investigate the impact of LBA on mobile users' behavior, specifically their reaction to watching attractive videos. This leads to important quantitative findings on how the battery level is coupled with the mobile video watching behavior, and these findings provide valuable guidances for mobile video streaming services.
- Based on our observations and findings through quantitative analysis and modeling, we give lessons and advice to mobile manufactures about HBI strategies and battery interfaces, to app developers/providers about energy-efficient mobile applications and mobile video streaming services.

2.2 Related Work

Existing investigations can be found relevant to battery use and recharge behavior of mobile users, including *qualitative* study in large-scale[1] [7, 19] or *quantitative* study in small-scale [16–18]. Nevertheless, no much attention has been paid to the emerging LBA issue. Our work is the first to conduct a both *large-scale* and *quantitative* study specifically on LBA and its impacts.

Large-Scale Qualitative Studies In 2016, LG conducted a survey among 2000 smartphone users in U.S., in which they found that: "nine out of 10 people 'felt panic' when their phone battery drops to 20% or lower" [7]. The phrase "low-battery anxiety" was firstly used in their survey report and caught a lot of attention. Thereafter, a successive relevant reports and news showed up in the press, especially recently. This indicates an awaking public concern towards the LBA issue. Nevertheless, no quantitative analysis and models were disclosed, and there is no measure to quantify the anxiety degree and its impact. A study of battery charging behaviors with 4035 participants was conducted in [19]. The battery information of

---

[1] The scale of study is debatable, since there is no broadly-accepted threshold counting for the large scale. We consider a study of sample size greater than 1000 people as large scale.

participants was collected via an Android application. Some statistical values were computed with the collected data, e.g., the average battery level, charging duration, charging schedule and frequency, based on which the authors obtained some charging behavior of participants, e.g., most users chose to interrupt the charging cycle which potentially reduces the battery life, and consistently overcharged their phones and tended to keep the battery levels above 30%. Nevertheless, neither quantitative models (beyond the statistical values) nor specific findings related to the LBA were provided.

Small-Scale Quantitative Studies In [17], the authors conducted a survey among high school students and collected 350 valid responses, among which only 41% of the respondents were mobile users with average age of 17 years old. According to the survey questionnaire, only qualitative self-estimation of LBA was performed. A small-group field study was also performed, in which the authors found that the mobile users could be categorized into two types regarding their charging behavior and they often have insufficient knowledge of the phone power characteristics. Although additional quantitative analysis on users' charging behavior was given, the field study was only made among 21 mobile users. The focused small student group may limit the generality and accuracy of the conclusions drawn from the survey. In [16], both questionnaire studies and handset monitoring were performed, on users' attitudes to mobile devices' energy and their behavior on battery recharge. The studies involved up to 253 participants, whose charging behavior was quantitatively analysed. The major findings include: most mobile users were good in estimating the energy consumption of mobile services, most mobile users were aware of power-saving settings and alters, and the mobile users demonstrated significant variation in battery use and recharge behavior. The anxiety caused by low-battery status, however, was not discussed in this work. In [18], the battery traces of 56 laptops and 10 mobile phones were collected and used to study the battery use and recharge behavior. The study yielded three major findings: (1) users frequently recharged their devices even when the battery power level is not low, (2) the charging behavior was driven by context or battery levels, and (3) there were significant variations in patterns shown by the users. Based on the user study, the authors designed a battery energy management system, called Llama, to enhance existing energy management policies. Nevertheless, the number of participants is too small to draw a reliable conclusion with respect to LBA.

2.3 A Survey Over 2000+ Mobile Users

To investigate the severity of LBA and quantify its impacts on mobile users, we (1) carefully designed a well-informed questionnaire (refer to the Appendix), (2) extensively distributed it over a popular mobile social network platform [20], and (3) continuously conducted the survey for over three months. At the end, we collected feedback from 2071 mobile users. After the data cleansing, we eventually obtained 2032 effective answers.

From the large-scale investigation, we obtained the information of (1) participants and mobile phones, (2) user satisfaction of mobile phone battery, and (3) severity of low-battery anxiety, details of which are described in Tables A.1, A.2 and A.3, respectively. Specifically, given the definition and "symptoms" of LBA, for the eighth question (Q8), the participants were required to self-estimate the severity of LBA they were suffering, especially when they were under inconvenient charging situations. Based on the feedback, it is surprising that 91.88% of the participants are suffering from the LBA, more or less. This is consistent with LG's survey [7], but the percentage is even higher in ours. Particularly, over 34% of them firmly admitted their suffering of LBA, with 6.10% of which claimed "severely suffering".

To this end, we can almost conclude that the LBA among mobile users are severe. It could also be confirmed with the feedback from Q6 and Q7. In the next section, we conduct a more thorough investigation on the LBA.

2.4 Quantification of Low-Battery Anxiety

Quantifying the LBA of mobile users is tricky. It is (methodologically) infeasible and (technically) inaccurate to ask a user to provide a real value representing her/his anxiety degree at each battery level. Thus, in our user survey, instead of directly asking for the anxiety degree, we turn to ask the battery level at which the user will charge the mobile phone, and then extract an LBA curve from the feedback of all participants.

2.4.1 Extraction of LBA Curve

Specifically, the ninth question (Q9) of our questionnaire is set as: *at what battery level (in percentage from 0 to 100%) will you charge your mobile phone, when it is possible?* The answer provides us with an angle to infer at which energy level the user begins to worry about the battery life, i.e., experience the low-battery anxiety. With all the answers from the 2032 participants, we are able to extract an empirical *LBA curve* by reversely accumulating over the histogram (showing the frequency at which users begin to experience the low-battery anxiety) and normalizing the cumulative numbers to [0, 1]. The detailed procedure is as follows:

1. **Initializing**: We first set 100 empty bins, labelled from 1 to 100, indicating the battery levels from (almost) empty to full;
2. **Counting**: For each of the answer, e.g., a (an integer in the region of [1, 100]), we add one to each of the bins with labels in [1, a];

Algorithm 1: LBA degree extraction (reversed accumulation of the charging threshold distribution)

Input: $inputs\_Q9$, the vector consisting of Q9 answers of all N participants.
Output: $anxiety\_degree$, the vector of anxiety degrees, corresponding to battery levels
       from 1 to 100%.
```
# (1) Initializing
```
$counter = [0 \textbf{ for } i \text{ in range}(100)]$
```
# (2) & (3): Counting & Cumulating
```
for $value$ in $inputs\_Q9$ **do**
    | **for** j in range($value$) **do**
    | | $counter[j] = counter[j] + 1$
```
# (4) Normalizing
```
$anxiety\_degree = [count/N \textbf{ for } count \text{ in } counter]$
return $anxiety\_degree$

---

3. **Cumulating**: We conduct the above operation for all answers and get the 100 bins with cumulative numbers, resulting in a declined (discrete) curve in the region of [1, 100];
4. **Normalizing**: By normalizing the cumulative numbers to [0, 1] to represent the anxiety degree, we obtain the LBA curve: *battery level* vs. *anxiety degree*.

The pseudocode of the above process is given in Algorithm 1 (in the *Python* programming style). Note that although the LBA degree extraction process seems simple, it is the result of a reverse-engineering idea and corresponding questionnaire design. Specifically, to learn the anxious degree curve of the mobile user with just one question, the question requires to make indications across different battery levels. By implicitly asking when a user begins to feel anxious about her/his battery power (i.e., the charging threshold), we are able to harvest the anxiety indications across all battery levels of the user, theoretically by a 0-1 binary vector with 0 indicating "not anxious" and 1 the opposite. Then, using a reversed accumulation approach among the 2000+ collected answers (distinguished from the standard histogram plotting approach), the empirical LBA curve (anxious degrees vs. battery levels) can thus be derived.

2.4.2 Observations and Analysis

2.4.2.1 Overall LBA Curve

The extracted LBA curve for all the participants is shown in Fig. 2.1, and the detailed values of anxiety degrees under different battery levels are listed in the Appendix. From the resulted LBA curve, we can observe that:

- The anxiety degree does not linearly increase with the decrease of battery level. As a comparison, we draw a straight line in Fig. 2.1 (i.e., the grey dashed

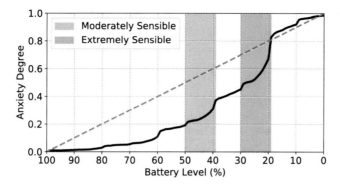

Fig. 2.1 Extracted LBA curve (the black solid line) from the survey data of 2032 mobile users, where the anxiety sensible regions are highlighted in orange and red

line), indicating the linear increase situation. It can be found that, the LBA curve is (approximately) convex to the battery level in [20%, 100%], while is (approximately) concave when the battery level drops to [0, 20%]. This observation shows that, the mobile user gets more sensible to the battery level as the energy drains.

- Two sensible regions of the users' anxiety can be found, named *moderately sensible* and *extremely sensible* regions as illustrated in Fig. 2.1, both corresponding to about 10% battery level drop. In the moderately sensible region, the 10% battery level dropping leads to 18% anxiety degree increases (from 0.19 to 0.37), while in the extremely sensible region the number is 38% (from 0.45 to 0.83). The occur of the extremely sensible region is most probably due to the battery user interface (e.g., the battery icon's color changes to yellow or red) and the low-battery warning message from the mobile OS.

2.4.2.2   LBA Curves for Different Age Groups

We further partition the participants into two groups: younger users aged between 18 and 35, and older users aged above 35. We then extract the LBA curves for the two groups respectively. The results are illustrated in Fig. 2.2, from which we find that:

- When battery levels are in regions of [25%, 40%], [45%, 60%] and [65%, 90%], the younger users are significantly more anxious about their mobile phones' battery levels than the older users (*all* $p < 0.05$).[2] This makes sense, as nowadays the younger users spend more time and thus are more dependent on the mobile phone than the older users.

---

[2] A $P \leq 0.05$ is considered as statistically significant for the purpose of this study.

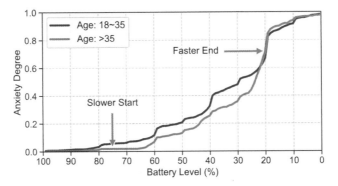

Fig. 2.2 LBA curves for different user age groups. The "slower start" and "faster end" characters can be found in the anxiety curve of the user group older than 35, compared with the younger users aged between 18 and 35

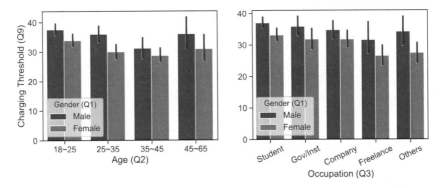

Fig. 2.3 Role of gender on the battery charging threshold, for user groups with different ages and occupations, respectively, from which we can find that females charge their mobile phones significantly earlier than males ($p = 0.05$)

- When the battery level is low (e.g., in the region of (0, 20%]), the older users start getting more sensible to the dropping of battery level, and their anxiety goes up rapidly and becomes higher than that of the younger users. The overall anxiety of the older users shows "slower start" and "faster end" phenomena, compared with that of the younger users.

2.4.2.3 Role of Gender in Battery Charging

In addition to the overall and age-respective analysis of the LBA curve, we also explore the roles of different human features in battery charging. One apparent finding is about the difference brought by gender. With the results illustrated in Fig. 2.3, we find that females charge their mobile phones (i.e., get anxious about the battery level) significantly earlier than males ($p = 0.05$), regardless of age and occupation. A similar conclusion was given in [21], where females had a higher score associated with the (negative) impact of nomophobia due to the problematic use of mobile phones.

2.4.3 Lessons Learnt from LBA Quantification

• To the developer/provider of energy-efficient or low-power applications/services: The LBA curve could be utilized to improve users' quality of experience (QoE), and the users staying in sensible regions could be the potential targets, compared to those in insensible regions. For example, in the work of [22], the authors adopted a similar idea to improve the user QoE of web service, by identifying and utilizing users' most sensible region for the webpage loading delay.
• To the mobile phone manufactures and mobile OS developers: During the designs of HBI strategy and battery interface, they should pay attention to the anxiety sensible regions, especially the extremely sensible one. Some measures, e.g., more efficient energy management strategies and considerate GUI designs, could be taken to smooth the curve (thus soothe the anxiety) in these regions. Furthermore, the younger mobile users may need more attention mainly due to their continuous higher anxiety over the battery lifetime. Some adaptations of the battery interface could be made, e.g., releasing sufficient information about the remaining battery energy or providing accurate and personalized battery lifetime predictions, to alleviate the anxiety and improve QoE.

2.5 Impacts of LBA on Video Watching

In this section, we investigate the impacts of LBA on mobile user's behavior, and specifically we are interested to see the mobile user's reaction in watching videos (i.e., during video streaming) when experiencing different levels of low-battery anxiety.

2.5.1 Extraction of Video Abandoning Likelihood Curve

In the last question (Q10) of our questionnaire, we ask the participants to answer: *at what battery level (in percentage from 1 to 100%) will you give up watching a*

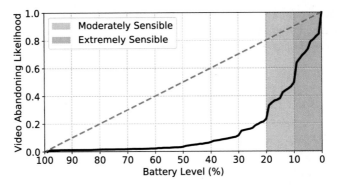

Fig. 2.4 The extracted video abandoning likelihood curve (the black solid line) from the survey data of 2032 mobile users. The video abandoning sensible regions are highlighted in orange and red

video you are interested in, when you are browsing the WeChat Moment or Weibo[3]*?* The feedback to this question directly shows how the mobile users value the battery power versus attractive videos, thus indicates how the LBA impacts the behavior of video watching.

Following a similar way of extracting the LBA curve (i.e., Algorithm 1, with $inputs\_Q9$ replaced by $inputs\_Q10$), we were able to extract a curve (illustrated in Fig. 2.4) called *video abandoning likelihood*. The curve actually indicates the likelihood[4] that a user may abandon video watching under different battery levels. From another perspective, the curve depicts the (approximate) proportion of mobile user, among the whole population, that will give up watching attractive videos at specific battery levels.

2.5.2 Observations and Analysis

2.5.2.1 Overall Video Abandoning Likelihood

The detailed values of video abandoning likelihood under different battery levels are provided in the Appendix. According to the video abandoning likelihood curve in Fig. 2.4, we have the following observations.

- The video abandoning likelihood does not linearly increase with the draining of battery power. In contrast, the curve is way below the linear trend (the grey

---

[3] The *WeChat Moment* and *Weibo* are currently the two biggest mobile social network platforms in China with billions of users. Tons of fresh and popular videos are shared there and updated by second.

[4] Note that this is not probability, as the integral below the curve is not equal to one.

dashed line in the figure), indicating that mobile users generally value attractive videos much more than the battery energy.

- When the battery level is above 20%, the user's video watching behavior seems not much affected by the battery level, with a video abandoning likelihood less than 0.23. Nevertheless, when the battery level drops below 20%, the video abandoning likelihood rises up quickly. Specifically, when the battery energy is left around 10%, nearly half (49.60%) of the mobile users will give up watching (attractive) videos.
- Two sensible regions of the video abandoning likelihood curve can be found: the *moderately sensible region* for battery level in [10%, 20%], corresponding to an abandoning likelihood increase of 0.26; the *extremely sensible region* for battery level in (0, 10%], corresponding to an abandoning likelihood increase of 0.50.

2.5.2.2 Video Abandoning Likelihood for Different Age Groups

We further partition the users into two groups: younger users with ages between 18 and 35, and older users with age above 35. Then, we extract the video abandoning likelihood curves for both groups. The results are illustrated in Fig. 2.5, from which we can find:

- The older users value the battery power more than the younger users. The video abandoning likelihood of older users is larger than that of the younger users, significantly when the battery level is low ([10%, 30%], $p = 0.05$). This copes with the fact that younger users spend more time on mobile apps (including video watching) than older users [23].
- Specifically, the largest gap between the two curves appears at the battery level of 17%, with video abandoning likelihoods of 0.54 and 0.33, respectively. This indicates that, when the battery energy drops to 17%, over 60% more users aged above 35 than those between 18 and 35 will give up watching attractive videos.

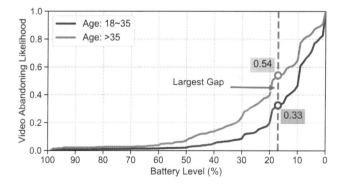

Fig. 2.5 The video abandoning likelihood under different age groups

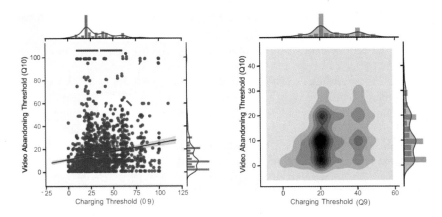

Fig. 2.6 (Left) the overall regression plot of correlation between charging threshold (Q9) and video abandoning threshold (Q10). (Right) the density plot of correlation between charging threshold (Q9) and video abandoning threshold (Q10). A zoomed-in view only for those with charging threshold $\leq 60\%$ and video abandoning threshold $\leq 40\%$

2.5.2.3 Correlation Between Battery Charging and Video Abandoning

We also perform a correlation analysis between users' feedback of the last two questions: battery charging threshold (Q9) vs. video abandoning threshold (Q10). Figure 2.6 shows the regression plot and density plot, along with the histograms (and corresponding density contours) at the margins. Based on the figure, we have the following findings:

- As shown on the left of Fig. 2.6, across the whole region of battery level from 0 to 100%, there is a weak positive (linear) correlation between users' charging thresholds and their video abandoning thresholds (Pearson's $r = 0.18$, $p < 0.01$).[5]
- From the density draw of the right of Fig. 2.6, we can see that when the battery level is low, a stronger correlation between the two answers can be found (Pearson's $r = 0.25$, $p < 0.01$). In particular, most users feel the low-battery anxiety (with intention to charge the mobile phone) when the battery level drops to around 20%, and thereafter they are likely to give up watching attractive videos for energy saving.

---

[5] Pearson correlation value is widely used to measure the linear correlation between two variables, which has a value region of $[-1, 1]$ with 1 denoting the strongest positive relationship and -1 the negative.

2.5.3 Advice for Video Streaming Services

The above observations and findings reveal important information for mobile video streaming services. Besides the traditional QoE metrics of video streaming, e.g., latency and resolution, the energy status of users' mobile phone should also be taken as a critical QoE metric. More attention should be drawn to the mobile users with battery level in the sensible regions, especially those in the extremely sensible region with battery level below 10%. If no measures were taken to alleviate the low-battery anxiety, the service provider may lose those customers. Furthermore, if the major potential customers of a video streaming service are mobile users aged above 35, the provider should take more efforts in alleviating the customers' low-battery anxiety.

There are already some work on energy-aware or low-power video streaming, based on optimization techniques or software/hardware technologies. For example, the display component of the mobile phone consumes a large portion of the total energy, especially when playing videos. Thus, researchers have developed sophisticated schemes to scale the display backlight or transform the video content, so that the display power consumption could be reduced [24]. To further cut down the mobile phone's energy consumption, the computation of video transform work can be mitigated to the cloud or edge servers [25]. The above energy-aware or low-power video streaming work could alleviate the low-battery anxiety and improve user QoE in mobile video streaming services.

2.6 Ethics

Before participating the survey, each mobile user was informed of the intention of this study, the course of data collection and processing, and how the data would be used. The participation is purely voluntary. We only collected data that are necessary for our analysis and quantification of low-battery anxiety, and all the data were anonymized without users' personal identification. Overall, our study would not cause privacy and ethics concerns.

2.7 Conclusion

In this work, we conducted a large-scale survey over 2000+ mobile users regarding the LBA issue and extracted quantitative models of LBA from the survey data. Through the survey investigation and LBA quantification, we revealed the severity of LBA among modern mobile users, quantified the anxiety degree of mobile users under varying battery levels, and quantified the impacts of LBA on mobile users' video watching behavior. The findings and lessons provided in this work could serve as valuable guidances in enhancing (1) the effectiveness of HBI strategies and battery interfaces and (2) the user QoE of mobile applications and services.

Chapter 3
User Energy and LBA Aware Mobile Video Streaming

3.1 Introduction

Evidence has shown that low-battery anxiety (or LBA, the fear of losing mobile phone battery power) can make wide impacts on the behavior of mobile users. According to our survey, over 20% of the mobile audiences will drop video watching when the battery life remains 20% and the dropping rate quickly rises to 50% when only 10% battery energy is left. This suggests that, saving mobile phone energy and prolonging its working time can not only release the suffering of LBA but also help customer retention in mobile video streaming services. For this purpose, we need to quantitatively investigate LBA and treat it as an important quality of experience (QoE) metric.

By looking into the power consumption splitting of the mobile platform during video streaming, we have found that the display module is the primary energy guzzler. As illustrated in Fig. 3.1, LCD and OLED, the mainstreams for smartphone displays, consume much higher energy than other components during the video playback. Although many efforts have been devoted to saving energy of the major components of mobile phones, e.g., CPU [10, 27] and communication module [11, 28], the energy consumption of the display has attracted relatively less attention.

Pushed by recent industrial developments, the percentage of energy consumption in displays may become even higher. First, with a continuous hardware upgrade, both the size and resolution of mobile displays are increasing. The display with

© The Author(s), under exclusive license to Springer Nature Singapore Pte Ltd. 2022
G. Tang et al., *GreenEdge: New Perspectives to Energy Management and Supply in Mobile Edge Computing*, SpringerBriefs in Computer Science,
https://doi.org/10.1007/978-981-16-9690-9_3

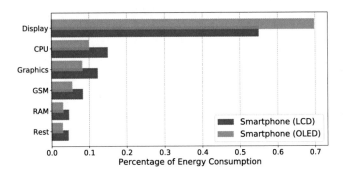

Fig. 3.1 Energy consumption of different hardware components of a smartphone during video playback (data for LCD smartphone is from [4], and data for OLED smartphone is estimated by comparing the power consumption of OLED and that of LCD [31])

a bigger size and a higher resolution has more pixels to power, compared to the smaller and lower-resolution one, thus making it more power hungry (e.g., the DELL XPS laptop display [29]). Second, 5G communications and edge computing [9, 30] are around the corner. Together, they promise the mobile users a much improved experience of (HD, 4K, or 8K) video watching, with faster speed, more stable connection, and lower latency than those of 4G networks. This in turn will further boom the already popular mobile video streaming services and lead to a much increased power consumption of displays.

Opportunities It has been found that different multimedia contents, represented by RGB pixel values, have quite different power dissipation on display (Sect. 3.2.2 for more details). This observation directly leads to the design of power-efficient image/video playing schemes using content transforming methods. With video transforming, a great portion of energy can be saved with negligible video quality distortion for human perception [24, 32]. While the image/video transforming can save display energy, it incurs extra CPU/GPU computation cost if performed on the mobile devices [24, 32]. Specifically, the transforming is operated on a per-pixel basis and thus computation intensive, especially for high-resolution displays. In consequence, the expected energy saving on mobile devices can be offset or even negated.

The emerging edge computing paradigm is an efficient way to interact with mobile devices at the network edge [33], by providing time-sensitive mobile services with computation, storage, and bandwidth resources close to the end users. Compared to the remote cloud, edge computing is a better choice for performing video transforming, since (1) video transforming depends on users' device types, e.g., backlight scaling for LCD and color transforming for OLED, and (2) edge server is much closer to mobile users. By leveraging edge computing for video transforming, we can save the display energy of mobile devices without the transforming overhead. We name such a refined service for low-power video streaming as LPVS, which could be provided as a value-added service by the mobile service provider.

Challenges There are some major challenges in the LPVS design. First, precisely quantifying the low-battery anxiety of mobile users is difficult and currently has no readily-available references. As the anxiety of mobile users belongs to one of the human feelings or emotions, it is not easy to measure (with some existing metric) nor optimize as we wished. Thus, without referred LBA metrics, *how can we measure and model the low-battery anxiety of mobile users in a quantitative way?* Second, due to limited computation resources at the edge environment, the video streaming provider may not be able to serve all but part of the audiences with video transforming. Taking the Nokia AirFrame open edge server [34] for example and referring to the video transcoding cost [35], one edge server can only process video streaming for about one hundred mobile devices simultaneously. Hence, under the resource constraint, *how can we choose the best subset of users to reduce their LBA?* To be specific, as most probably the LBA is not linearly increased with the draining of battery power, *how can we accommodate the quantified low-battery anxiety and choose the most cost-effective user groups for video transforming?* Additionally, as the LBA models of mobile users under different circumstances might be different, *is there any way to update the model, such that the renewed model could capture more about the LBA features under a specific circumstance.*

Contributions Addressing the above challenges, this chapter systematically and quantitatively investigates the problem of alleviating LBA of mobile users. The innovation is to use LBA as a critical performance metric to guide video transforming at the edge. This work includes the following contributions:

- We conduct a large-scale survey over 2000+ mobile users on low-battery anxiety, to model the quantitative relationship between the mobile users' anxiety degree and the mobile devices' battery status. This survey and corresponding empirical conclusions provide strong real-world evidences on the importance of this work.
- By incorporating the extracted quantitative model of LBA, we propose a new solution tailored for low-power video streaming, named LPVS, in which we explicitly depict the scenario and systematically model the energy saving and anxiety reduction by a joint optimization problem. By analyzing the hardness of the optimization problem, we further develop a two-phase heuristic method to solve it using information compacting and Bayesian inference.
- To accommodate the LBA heterogeneity of mobile users under various circumstances, we further design an LBA model updating scheme for specific edge environments. The updating scheme takes the unique characteristics of mobile users at local circumstances into consideration and thus is expected to achieve more realistic LBA models.
- We develop the LPVS emulator and use a real-world *Twitch* dataset to evaluate the performance of LPVS. Extensive emulation results demonstrate that, with LPVS, the overall mobile users can save their devices' energy by up to 37% (thus much reducing the LBA of mobile users) and those low-battery users can prolong their video watching time by 39%.

3.2 Background and Related Work

3.2.1 Background of Low-Battery Anxiety

The anxiety caused by the low battery power of handheld devices has been noticed for a long time. It was initially investigated under the cover of *nomophobia*, which refers to the fear of being without a smartphone. In 2016, LG performed a survey of 2000 smartphone users in the US. The survey found that 19% of the mobile users would "feel panic" when their phone battery drops to 20% or lower [7]. Since then, the low-battery anxiety, i.e., LBA, has been widely known to the public.

LBA can bring widely and deeply negative impacts on mobile users' lives. According to the LG's survey, one in three people is likely to skip the gym, when it comes to choosing between hitting the gym and charging their smartphones. Furthermore, for those severely suffering from the LBA, it can cause strange behaviors, e.g., head home immediately, ask for chargers from strangers, or secretly "borrow" other's charger. To be even worse, LBA is becoming the major trigger of nomophobia, which is commonly treated as one type of mental health problem.

Although LBA has shown negative effects upon mobile users' emotions, behavior, and even health, it has not been investigated thoroughly. To be specific, there is no prior work measuring and quantifying LBA in a quantitative way, which is one of the major tasks in this work.

3.2.2 Background of Display Power Saving

Modern smartphones are typically equipped with one of the two display types: Liquid-Crystal Displays (LCD) or Organic Light-Emitting Diode (OLED) displays. The two types of displays work differently and have quite different power consumption characteristics.

3.2.2.1 Power Saving for LCD

The major power consumer of LCD is its backlight, which illuminates the liquid crystals of the display with various brightness levels. Its power consumption can be quite different at different brightness levels. Thus, by strategically scaling the backlight and regulating the image luminance, the original image displayed by an LCD can be rendered with much less energy and a distortion negligible/tolerable for human perception [24]. Accordingly, a broad spectrum of schemes based on backlight scaling (with luminance compensation) have been proposed to cut down the power consumption of LCD.

3.2.2.2 Power Saving for OLED

Compared to LCD, the OLED display is not only thinner and lighter, but also can support up to three orders of magnitude higher refresh rates [36]. For the OLED display, different RGB color sub-pixels generate lights with different energy efficiencies: the blue pixels consume about twice the power of green ones, while the red in between of the two [12]. Thus, the power consumption much relies on the displayed colors (rather than the brightness). On the other hand, the human visual system (HVS) has a great perceptual flexibility, thus can tolerate small color changes [12]. Accordingly, various color transforming schemes have been developed for saving energy of OLED displays.

We summarize existing strategies for display power saving in Table 3.1, for the LCD and OLED displays, respectively. Nevertheless, these strategies are "pixel-wise", i.e., they operate on a per-pixel basis, which incurs a non-negligible overhead for the mobile devices, especially those with high-resolution displays [24, 32].

3.2.3 Work Related to This Work

Since our work aims at offloading the computation intensive image/video transforming from smartphones to edge servers to keep users from worrying about quick battery drainage, we first introduce the relevant work on proxy-based display energy saving for video streaming. Then we investigate recent work on energy-performance tradeoff in the edge/cloud environment, which is the essential problem tackled in this work.

Table 3.1 Review of the state-of-the-art power saving strategies for LCD and OLED, respectively

Type	Applied strategy	Power saving
LCD	Quality adapted backlight scaling [37]	27–42%
	Dynamic backlight scaling [38]	15–49%
	Dynamic backlight luminance scaling [39]	20–80%
	Brightness and contrast scaling [40]	≤50%
	Luminance dimming and compensation [41]	20–38%
OLED	Color and shape transforming [12]	25–66%
	Color transforming and darkening [25]	≤60%
	Color transforming with constraints [32]	≤64%
	Pixel disabling and resolution scaling [42]	≤26%
	Image pixel scaling [43]	38–42%
	Redundant subpixel shutoff [44]	≤21%
Average		13–49%

3.2.3.1 Proxy-Based Energy Saving

In [37], by analyzing the characteristics of video streaming services, the authors proposed a quality adapted backlight scaling scheme for LCD energy saving during video playback of handheld devices. In their prototype, a proxy server was set up for video transforming and over 40% of the energy saving was achieved. A similar idea was applied in the work of [45], where the adaptation of video transforming was shifted from the low-power device to a proxy middleware. In both work, the proxy server is a testing platform designed for one dedicated client device, which is different from our scenario where the video streaming service is provided for a group of users. Above all, neither of them takes the users' low-battery anxiety into consideration, which is another major difference from our work.

3.2.3.2 Energy-Performance Tradeoff

For the tradeoff between energy and latency in vehicular fog computing, the author in [46] presented a dynamic computation offloading and resources allocation scheme (ECOS). the ECOS was formulated as a joint energy and latency cost minimization problem, and a heuristic approach was then developed to tackle the optimization problem. Similarly, in mobile cloud computing, the author of [47] designed an adaptive heuristics energy-aware approach to detecting overload hosts and selecting VMs for consolidation. The goal was to jointly minimize total energy consumption and maximize the QoS (in terms of SLA violations).

3.3   LBA Survey and Modelling

Note that more detailed LBA survey and modelling processes are introduced in Chap. 2. The reader can skip this section if they have already read the previous chapter.

3.3.1   Data Collection

To learn the impact of low-battery anxiety and establish a quantitative model, we carefully designed an online survey (refer to Appendix A for the detailed questionnaire) and continuously collected the answers from mobile users for over three months. In the end, we collected 2032 effective answers after data cleansing. Refer to Appendix A for detailed information regarding the participants.

Based on the survey data, it is surprising that 91.88% (1867 out of 2032) of the participants are suffering from the low-battery anxiety, more or less. This is consistent with the LG survey [7], but the percentage is even higher in our survey.

It is also interesting to see that nearly half of the mobile users will give up watching an attractive video, once the battery level of mobile phone drops below 10%. These findings provide direct and strong support to the necessity of our work.

3.3.2 LBA Curve Extraction

In our elaborately designed questionnaire, one question the participants need to answer is: *At what battery level (in percentage from 0 to 100%) will you charge your mobile phone, when it is possible?* The answers provide us with an angle to infer at which energy level a user normally begins to worry about the battery life, i.e., experience the low-battery anxiety. Then, with all the collected answers, we are able to extract the LBA curve model: the anxiety degree (caused by the draining of battery power) vs. the battery energy status.

Specifically, a four-step procedure is conducted to obtain the LBA curve from the raw data: (1) initialize 100 empty bins, indicating the battery level from (almost) empty to full (i.e., [1, 100]); (2) for each answer, e.g., a (an integer in [1, 100]), add one to each of the bins in [1, a]; (3) conduct (2) for all the answers and obtain a declined discrete curve in the region of [1, 100]; (4) normalize the 100 cumulative numbers to the region of [0, 1], denoting the anxiety degree, we obtain the LBA curve: anxiety degree vs. battery level. A similar approach was also adopted in [48], to identify the commonly used response time thresholds for service level objectives in cloud service.

Following the above extraction process, the resulting LBA curve from the surveyed 2032 users is shown in Fig. 3.2. From the illustrated LBA curve, we can observe that:

- The anxiety degree does not linearly increase with the decrease of energy level. If we use the linear function (the straight dashed line in Fig. 3.2) as a comparison, the user's anxiety is a convex function of the energy level when the energy level is in [20%, 100%], but is concave when the energy level drops to [0, 20%].

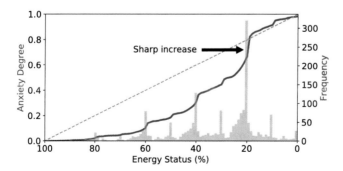

Fig. 3.2 Extracted anxiety curve from the survey data of 2032 mobile users

- A sharp increase of anxiety can be observed when the energy level drops to 20%. This is most probably caused by the color change of battery icon (e.g., the icon's face color changes to yellow or red) and the low-battery warning message.

Notice that moderate increases of anxiety can be observed at the energy levels of 40 and 60%. This might be caused by the participants' rough estimations made on a decimal base, when filling out questionnaires. For example, instead of a specific number, one may tend to fill an approximate number like 20, 40, or 60.

3.3.3   Insights on LBA Alleviation

The non-linearity of the LBA curve indicates that, the user's sensitivity to the power draining (at different battery levels) is heterogeneous. This also implies that, when choosing a subset of mobile users for anxiety minimizing, following a random user selection strategy cannot be optimal, as those who are currently not sensitive to the energy status may be selected (thus resulting in less performance gain). Instead, the mobile users that are sensitive to the battery power draining, e.g., those near the "sharp increase" area in Fig. 3.2, should be given a higher priority. This is also how our optimization scheme will take effect (Sect. 3.4.5).

Note that the extracted LBA curve was obtained with survey questions, with the assumption that participants' answers truthfully reflect their feelings and behaviors. This assumption may be challenged. An alternative method to avoid this pitfall is to look into users' real behaviors [49, 50]. Later in Sect. 3.6, we will introduce a local LBA model updating scheme to renew the original LBA information, based on the events when the mobile users charge their phones and circumstances where the mobile users locate, making the LBA curve as accurate as possible.

3.4   LPVS: Low-Power Video Streaming

3.4.1   Scenario Overview

Content delivery networks (CDN) [51] have been broadly adopted for video delivery. A CDN consists of CDN servers that are close to end users and cache content for fast video delivery. Nowadays, CDN is integrated with edge computing technology to push the content even closer to end users. As illustrated by Fig. 3.3, we assume the 5G mobile edge computing (MEC) [30] platform consisting of 5G base stations, edge servers, and CDN servers, where the 5G base stations and edge servers are deployed at locations close to end users and the CDN servers are located at the CDN Point of Presence (PoP). There is a content delivery strategy between the edge servers and the CDN servers [52, 53], which may prefetch a certain amount of video content from the CDN servers to the edge server, based on the (historical) video

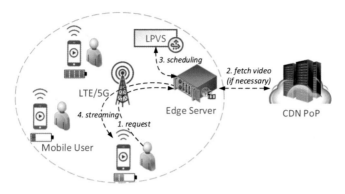

Fig. 3.3 The procedure of LPVS within a virtual cluster at the edge

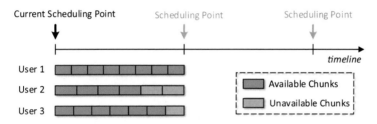

Fig. 3.4 Illustration of scheduling points and available/unavailable video chunks at three users' mobile devices

requests from the mobile users. This content prefetch strategy provides underlying support for and is independent of LPVS.

We assume that all the mobile devices within one region (e.g., the covered area of a base station) form one *virtual cluster* (VC), where they share the same edge server. Without loss of generality, assume that one VC hosts N mobile devices. We divide the time into slots of equal length (e.g., 5-minute interval in our implementation as per Remark 3.1). LPVS needs to make a (new) scheduling decision for video transforming at the beginning of each time slot (scheduling points in Fig. 3.4).

Usually, a complete video is split into a number of small chunks, but depending on different caching strategies [53], the edge server might not have the whole video chunks and the number of available video chunks may vary. For a video m, assume that the currently available number of video chunks, at the scheduling point, is K_m. With the above notations, we denote the video chunks played on device n in time slot t by $d_n(t)$, $1 \le n \le N, t \ge 1$, with:

$$d_n(t) := \langle VID, CID_1, \ldots, CID_{K_m} \rangle \qquad (3.1)$$

in which VID stands for the video ID and CID_i, $i = 1, \ldots, K_m$, for the IDs of video chunks available for device n at the beginning of time slot t.

Overall, at the scheduling point, LPVS should make decisions on whether or not the edge server should perform video transforming for certain users in the VC, to save display power and alleviate their low-battery anxiety.

Remark 3.1 We ignore the scenario where a user switches videos during one time slot. This omission is due to the periodical scheduling used in LPVS. The interval time should not be too small (e.g., in seconds) to avoid unnecessary computational overhead at the edge server. The empirical value of 5 minutes is used based on the facts that (1) battery level should not drop too much during this time and (2) people can tolerate a certain level of anxiety when battery level does not drop too much. If a user switches videos during one time slot, LPVS will keep the same decision (i.e., with or without video transforming) for this user until the next scheduling point.

3.4.2 Models for Power Consumption in Video Streaming

When a device plays a video, its *power rate*[1] may fluctuate up and down along with the played chunks, due to different brightness levels (for the LCD) or different color distributions (for the OLED). When playing video m, we denote the power rate on the n-th device for the κ-th chunk by $p_{n,m}(\kappa)$, $1 \leq n \leq N$, $1 \leq m \leq M$, $1 \leq \kappa \leq K_m$. Note that, given the display's specification (e.g., type, size, and resolution) and the available video chunk κ, corresponding power rate $p_{n,m}(\kappa)$ can be estimated with existing power models for LCD [39] or OLED [12].

Also notice that, within one time slot, the requested video chunks may be not all available (due to different prefetching and buffering strategies), as illustrated for user 2 and user 3 in Fig. 3.4. Under such a situation, we only use the available video chunks for the estimation of $p_{n,m}(\kappa)$.

By applying the video transforming (given in Sect. 3.2) on the video $d_n(t)$, the *power reduction ratio*[2] of a specific device n during the time slot t can be represented as $\gamma_n(d_n(t))$ (γ_n for simplicity), where $0 < \gamma_n < 1$. For different chunks of the same video, γ_n could be different, as the contents (e.g., RGB color pixels) of each chunk could be different. Thus, the value of γ_n is not constant during the video play.

Remark 3.2 We introduce γ_n to represent the average power saving ratio on device n, which has been achieved over a bunch of video chunks in one time slot. As its value can only be learnt after playing the transformed video, we use it as a random variable to keep track of the most recent power saving ratio of device n. Specifically, the Bayesian inference is applied to update the value of γ_n in Sect. 3.5.4. In the following part of modeling, we assume that we have already learnt the knowledge of γ_n.

---

[1] The power rate is defined as the energy consumption of the mobile device in the time of playing one video chunk.

[2] The power reduction rate is defined by the ratio of a device's power consumption with and without video transforming during one time slot.

At the beginning of an arbitrary time slot t, due to limited edge server capacity, LPVS may only choose a subset of requested videos for transforming. We denote the decision variable of whether to perform video transforming for the n-th device during the entire time slot by x_n, with $x_n = 1$ indicating yes and $x_n = 0$ otherwise. Thus, for the time slot t, we have:

$$x_n \in \{0, 1\}, \forall n. \tag{3.2}$$

By determining the value of x_n and referring to the knowledge of $p_{n,m}(\kappa)$ and γ_n, we are able to infer the power rate of device n when playing the κ-th chunk of video m by:

$$\psi_{n,m}(\kappa) = x_n \cdot \gamma_n \cdot p_{n,m}(\kappa) + (1 - x_n) \cdot p_{n,m}(\kappa), \forall n, \forall \kappa. \tag{3.3}$$

3.4.3 Models for Energy Status and Low-Battery Anxiety

Another important information in LPVS is the energy status of mobile devices, measured by the remaining energy of the battery. We denote the energy status of the n-th device at the beginning of an arbitrary time slot by $e_{n,m}(\kappa)$, where m and κ are the video ID and the video chunk ID, respectively, requested by the n-th device.

Before the edge server determines to transform a video chunk requested by device n, the device should have sufficient energy to power the device (otherwise the transforming has no meaning). Hence, the following inequality should hold:

$$e_{n,m}(\kappa) \geq x_n \cdot \gamma_n \cdot p_{n,m}(\kappa) \cdot \Delta_\kappa, \forall n, \forall \kappa, \tag{3.4}$$

where Δ_κ denotes the time length of current video chunk. Thus, when $x_n = 0$, i.e., the video chunks requested by device n are not transformed, the above inequality takes no effect (always holds), as $e_{n,m}(\kappa)$ is non-negative.

Meanwhile, with the power rate of device n when playing the κ-th chunk of video m (given by $\psi_{n,m}(\kappa)$ in (3.3)), the energy status of the device before playing the next video chunk $(\kappa + 1)$ can be predicted by:

$$e_{n,m}(\kappa + 1) = e_{n,m}(\kappa) - \psi_{n,m}(\kappa) \cdot \Delta_\kappa, \forall n, 1 \leq \kappa \leq K_m - 1. \tag{3.5}$$

As we have mentioned, over 90% of the mobile users are suffering from the low-battery anxiety [7] (the figure is 91.88% in our survey). Usually, the less the battery energy, the higher the anxiety. Such relationship between the battery energy status and the low-battery anxiety have been captured by the anxiety curve shown in Fig. 3.2.

We use $\phi(\cdot)$ to denote the empirical function reflecting the *anxiety degree* of a user given the energy status of his device. To be specific, for device n with the energy status of $e_{n,m}(\kappa)$, the anxiety degree of its owner can be estimated by $\phi(e_{n,m}(\kappa))$. As illustrated by Fig. 3.2, the anxiety degree of a user is between 0 and 1, with energy status of her mobile device between 100% and 0, correspondingly.

As has been reported, low-battery anxiety can potentially have a negative effect on user's video watching behavior (Sect. 3.3.1). Thus, we believe that reducing user's low-battery anxiety is a critical aspect in improving the QoE of video streaming service, which is one key feature of our LPVS.

3.4.4   Video Streaming Capacity at the Edge

For the video chunks requested by device n and to be transformed at the edge during time slot t (i.e., $d_n(t)$), the computing resource that the video transforming needs is estimated by $g(d_n(t))$, where $g(\cdot)$ is the function reflecting the server's computing resource needed for video transforming. Similarly, the storage resource that the video transforming consumes can be estimated by $h(d_n(t))$, where $h(\cdot)$ is a function for storage space measuring during video transforming.

For the edge server attached to a VC, it usually has quite limited computing and storage resources (e.g., the *NOKIA* or *Inspur* edge server [34, 54]). We denote the *extra* computing and storage resources available at the edge server to perform video transforming by C and S, respectively. Then we have the following two capacity constraints:

$$\sum_{n=1}^{N} x_n \cdot g(d_n(t)) \leq C, \tag{3.6}$$

$$\sum_{n=1}^{N} x_n \cdot h(d_n(t)) \leq S. \tag{3.7}$$

3.4.5   Joint Optimization for Energy Saving and Anxiety Reduction

Given the edge server capacity constraints, for each time slot, our targets are (1) to minimize the display energy consumption of all the mobile devices during video playback, and (2) to minimize the anxiety degree of all users simultaneously. The problem can be formulated as:

$$\min_{\{x_1, x_2, \cdots, x_N\}} \sum_{n=1}^{N} \sum_{\kappa=1}^{K_m} \left(\psi_{n,m}(\kappa) + \lambda \cdot \phi(e_{n,m}(\kappa)) \right) \tag{3.8a}$$

$$\text{s.t.} \qquad (3.2) \sim (3.7), \tag{3.8b}$$

where λ is a *regularization parameter* that balances the two targets, and K_m is a constant representing the total number of chunks processed by the video streaming server in one time slot (for an arbitrary video m).

Remark 3.3 In the practice of LPVS, the regularization parameter λ should be determined or regulated by the video streaming service providers, based on their own policies and specific service-level agreements (SLAs) with the customers. We will show how this parameter can affect the results, i.e., the energy saving and anxiety reduction, in Sect. 3.8.

3.5 Solution Methodology

3.5.1 The Difficulties

It is nontrivial to solve the joint optimization problem given by (3.8), mainly due to three difficulties:

Difficulty-1 The device energy status $(e_{n,m}(\kappa))$ should be predicted after playing each video chunk during the whole time slot, for constraints (3.3), (3.4) and (3.5) and the objective function. For instance, with the effect of κ, the energy status update with (3.5) needs to be performed chunk by chunk. The constraints and the objective function hence twist together, making the optimization problem hard to solve.

Difficulty-2 The problem generally belongs to the integer programming (as $x_n(t)$ is binary), while whether it is linear or nonlinear solely depends on the function of $\phi(\cdot)$ (i.e., the anxiety curve) in the objective (3.8a). Referring to our extracted anxiety curve in Fig. 3.2, the function is obviously not linear and thus the problem we are facing belongs to the nonlinear integer programming, which is normally intractable.

Difficulty-3 Different devices may have different power reduction ratios γ_n, whose value is unknown in advance. As we have mentioned, γ_n is not a fixed value and may vary over different transformed videos. Hence, it causes a *circular argument*: to solve the problem, we need the value of γ_n as one of the inputs; on the other hand, we may have no information about the value of γ_n before the problem is solved.

We tackle the above three difficulties with (1) information compacting, (2) a two-phase heuristic, and (3) Bayesian inference, respectively.

3.5.2 Information Compacting

We find that both the constraints and the objective can be compacted in a way that (1) κ is marginalized and (2) the intermediate energy status $(e_{n,m}(\kappa))$ is eliminated.

After information compacting, we can transform the problem into a neater form that renders an easy solution.

(1) Information Compacting for the Constraints
First, we perform information compacting on the constraints of (3.4) and (3.5), as only these two constraints relate to $e_{n,m}(\kappa)$. We first summarize over κ for the inequality of constraint (3.4):

$$\sum_{\kappa=1}^{K_m} e_{n,m}(\kappa) \geq x_n \gamma_n \sum_{\kappa=1}^{K_m} p_{n,m}(\kappa) \qquad (3.9)$$

Using (3.5), we rewrite the left-hand side of (3.9) as:

$$\sum_{\kappa=1}^{K_m} e_{n,m}(\kappa) \qquad (3.10a)$$

$$= e_{n,m}(1) + e_{n,m}(2) + \cdots + e_{n,m}(K_m) \qquad (3.10b)$$

$$= e_{n,m}(1) + \big(e_{n,m}(1) - \psi_{n,m}(1)\big) +$$
$$+ \big(e_{n,m}(1) - \psi_{n,m}(1) - \psi_{n,m}(2)\big) + \ldots \qquad (3.10c)$$

$$= K_m \cdot e_{n,m}(1) - \sum_{\kappa=1}^{K_m}(K_m - \kappa)\psi_{n,m}(\kappa) \qquad (3.10d)$$

Replacing the left-hand side of (3.9) with (3.10d), we have:

$$K_m \cdot e_{n,m}(1) - \sum_{\kappa=1}^{K_m}(K_m - \kappa)\psi_{n,m}(\kappa)$$

$$\geq x_n \gamma_n \sum_{\kappa=1}^{K_m} p_{n,m}(\kappa). \qquad (3.11)$$

In constraint (3.11), for given values of the decision variables x_n, $1 \leq n \leq N$, all the other parameters are easy to calculate:

- K_m: the total number of video chunks delivered within one time slot, which is a known constant for each individual video;
- $e_{n,m}(1)$: the initial energy status of each device at the beginning of each time slot, which is reported at the scheduling point by each device;
- $p_{n,m}(\kappa)$: the power rate of the device playing each chunk (without transforming), which is known beforehand with existing power models;
- $\psi_{n,m}(\kappa)$: the power rate of the device playing each chunk under the given value of decision variable x_n, which can be computed with the knowledge of $p_{n,m}(\kappa)$ (refer to the definition in (3.3));

- γ_n: the power reduction ratio of each device after video transforming, which can be estimated and updated via a Bayesian approach (refer to the details in Sect. 3.5.4).

(2) Information Compacting in Objective

Next, we perform information compacting for the objective function to avoid the computation of intermediate energy status $e_{n,m}(\kappa)$. With (3.5), we can derive the relationship between a device's predicted energy status (after playing a video chunk) and its initial energy status:

$$e_{n,m}(\kappa) \tag{3.12a}$$

$$= e_{n,m}(\kappa - 1) - \psi_{n,m}(\kappa - 1) \tag{3.12b}$$

$$= e_{n,m}(\kappa - 2) - \psi_{n,m}(\kappa - 2) - \psi_{n,m}(\kappa - 1) \tag{3.12c}$$

$$\vdots$$

$$= e_{n,m}(1) - \sum_{i=1}^{\kappa-1} \psi_{n,m}(i) \tag{3.12d}$$

Thus, the objective function (3.8a) can be rewritten as:

$$\sum_{n=1}^{N} \sum_{\kappa=1}^{K_m} \left(\psi_{n,m}(\kappa) + \lambda \cdot \phi(e_{n,m}(1) - \sum_{i=1}^{\kappa-1} \psi_{n,m}(i)) \right) \tag{3.13}$$

in which all the elements are either readily available or can be easily computed with the given decision variable of x_n.

We then apply the compacted constraint (3.11) to replace original constraints (3.4) and (3.5), and the transformed objective (3.13) to replace the original objective (3.8a). It is worth mentioning that the compacted form of the problem is equivalent to the original problem (3.8), as information compacting comes from (3.9) and (3.12), which only involve equalities.

3.5.3 A Two-Phase Heuristic for Joint Optimization

To solve the nonlinear integer problem, we develop a two-phase heuristic method:

- **Phase-1**: We solve the following optimization problem:

$$\min_{\{x_1, x_2, \cdots, x_N\}} \sum_{n=1}^{N} \sum_{\kappa=1}^{K_m} \psi_{n,m}(\kappa) \tag{3.14a}$$

$$\text{s.t.} \qquad (3.2), (3.6), (3.7), (3.11). \tag{3.14b}$$

Without considering the nonlinear function $\phi(\cdot)$, the above problem belongs to linear integer programming (ILP). Furthermore, with the compacted form, it can be directly fed into the off-the-shelf ILP solvers, such as CPLEX [55], Gurobi [56] or CVX [57]. By solving the problem, we actually obtain a subset (say, with the number of N') of the mobile devices for video transforming, with which the energy consumption is minimized.

- **Phase-2**: To further cope with users' anxiety, we sort the mobile devices by their energy status, with which the anxiety degrees of mobile users are ranked. Then, we try to swap the selected N' devices in Phase-1 with the first $(N - N')$ devices whose owners have the largest anxiety degrees. The swapping is successful only when the objective value computed with (3.13) is reduced. The nonlinear function $\phi(\cdot)$ could use an empirical function that reflects either (1) the global LBA varying characteristics of a large population as given in Sect. 3.3, or (2) the local LBA varying characteristics of the users within a specific VC as will be introduced in Sect. 3.6.

Note that the computational complexities of both Phase-1 and Phase-2 are much lower than solving the original nonlinear programming. For a VC including 1000 devices, our implementation on a low-end machine can find the optimal solution in Phase-1 in 5 seconds using the off-the-shelf ILP solver, and can finish the swapping process within 1 minute. Considering the scheduling time length is 5 minutes in our implementation, the computing overhead of LPVS is acceptable under the "one-slot-ahead" scheduling working mode, which means that during the current slot, the LPVS scheduler decides for the incoming requests in the next time slot.

3.5.4   Determine γ_n with Bayesian Inference

When playing a transformed video, mobile devices of different specifications (LCD or OLED, size, etc.) may have different power reduction ratios γ_n. Nevertheless, before a transformed video is played on device n, the value of γ_n is unknown. In other words, at a scheduling point, we actually do not know the value of γ_n for the following time slot (since the video chunks have not been played yet).

Although we cannot know the value of γ_n for the current time slot t ($t > 1$), fortunately we do have the information of the previous time slot $t - 1$ and can get the value of γ_n at the end of the previous time slot. This inspires us to update the value of γ_n with the obtained information (observation) from previous time slots. Such an idea can be naturally implemented with Bayesian inference, by treating γ_n as a random variable.

(1) At the Beginning of the 1st Time Slot
At the beginning of the first time slot, we initialize the probability distribution function (PDF) of power reduction ratio with a Gaussian distribution:

$$p(\gamma_n) = \mathcal{N}(\mu, \sigma^2) \tag{3.15}$$

where μ and σ^2 represent the mean and variance of the Gaussian distribution, respectively. μ can be initialized by:

$$\mu = \frac{\gamma_L + \gamma_U}{2}, \tag{3.16}$$

with γ_L and γ_U representing the lower and upper bounds of power reduction ratio, respectively (refer to Table 3.1). As to the initialization of σ^2, we can choose a relatively big value due to the lack of confidence about the concentration of γ_n, e.g., $\sigma^2 = 12$ in our implementation.

(2) At the End of Time Slot t

With the observation of power reduction when playing transformed video in time slot t, denoted by Δ_n, we update the PDF of γ_n for the next time slot by computing the posterior using the Bayesian rule:

$$p(\gamma_n|\Delta_n) = \frac{P(\Delta_n|\gamma_n)p(\gamma_n)}{P(\Delta_n)}, \tag{3.17}$$

where $p(\gamma_n)$ is the prior of γ_n used in time slot t; $P(\Delta_n|\gamma_n)$ is the likelihood of the observation under γ_n; $P(\Delta_n)$ is the marginal distribution of Δ_n over γ_n, i.e.,

$$P(\Delta_n) = \int_{\gamma_L}^{\gamma_U} P(\Delta_n|\gamma_n)p(\gamma_n)d\gamma_n. \tag{3.18}$$

(3) At the Beginning of Time Slot t + 1

With the above posterior of γ_n, we compute the expected value (or the expectation) of γ_n:

$$\mathbf{E}_{p(\gamma_n|\Delta_n)} = \int_{\gamma_L}^{\gamma_U} \gamma_n p(\gamma_n|\Delta_n)d\gamma_n, \tag{3.19}$$

and apply the obtained value for video transforming scheduling (i.e., $\gamma_n = \mathbf{E}_{p(\gamma_n|\Delta_n)}$) for time slot $t + 1$.

Note that, as γ_n is assumed to follow the Gaussian distribution, the likelihood-prior pair in (3.17) is conjugate.[3] In this way, the update of γ_n can be computed precisely without any approximation.

---

[3] A likelihood-prior pair is said to be conjugate if they result in a posterior that is of the same form as the prior.

3.6 LBA Model Updating

3.6.1 Analysis of LBA Heterogeneity

Naturally, the LBA models for user groups in different areas are different, due to the specific circumstances the users may face. For example, in a shopping mall area, the users tend to have no charging facilities and thus could follow our surveyed LBA model; whereas in the residential area, most probably the users have chargers at hand and thus might follow a much different LBA curve. In this work, we name such differences *heterogeneity* of the low-battery anxiety properties among mobile users.

Due to the heterogeneity, a global LBA model obtained through the large-scale user survey (as illustrated in Fig. 3.2) may not precisely reflect the LBA features that local mobile users (in a VC) adhere to. This motivates us to renew the already-obtained LBA model by further considering the charging behavior of mobile users under specific circumstances. Hence, we design a local LBA updating scheme based on the random charging-event sampling within each VC. We do not aim to provide personalized LBA models for individual users, as this will bring a huge cost for a large-scale population.

3.6.2 Local LBA Model Updating

The local LBA updating scheme is conducted at each edge server and meanwhile cooperated by the mobile users (or client ends) within each VC. We then introduce the detailed procedures for the client ends and the edge server, respectively, which are also illustrated in Fig. 3.5.

- At each Client End: (1) A charging event database (or event DB) is created by recording every plug-in charging event conducted by the mobile user, e.g., referring to the human-battery interaction APIs provided by the mobile OS or platform [16, 18]. (2) The event DB keeps a record of the charging events during the whole time of the mobile users using the mobile phone, no matter playing videos or not. (3) When playing videos, upon the request from the edge server, the client samples a number of (e.g., $q \geq 1$) charging events from the event DB and reports them to the edge server in the VC, by every time interval of Δ_s. As the battery API is offered by the mobile OS, it has little cost to obtain the charging events. The event DB will not occupy too much space, as normally a mobile user does not charge her/his phone frequently (e.g., $1 \sim 4$ a day in our survey). Thus, the overhead of keeping track of the charging events could be negligible.
- At the Edge Server: (1) The edge server first initializes its local LBA model (ϕ_0) using the obtained empirical one given in Fig. 3.2. (2) Then at the beginning of the i-th updating interval (of Δ_s), the edge server broadcasts charging event

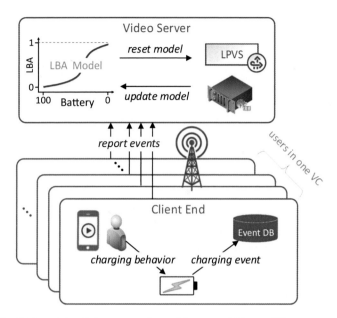

Fig. 3.5 The LBA model updating process for mobile users within one VC

requests to the active clients within the VC. (3) At the end of the i-th updating interval, with the collected charging events information, the edge server renews the (old) LBA model (ϕ_i), by borrowing the four-step procedure introduced in Sect. 3.3.2 and treating each charging event as an answer to the specified surveyed question. (4) The edge server resets the local LBA model by ϕ_i, which is then fed into the joint optimization model given in Sect. 3.5.

With the above local LBA model updating procedures at the edge server and its adhered clients, the new LBA curve is expected to reflect the specific LBA varying characteristics within each VC more precisely than the original global one extracted from the user survey.

Privacy Concern Since the charging events of each client could reveal her/his particular behavior characteristics, we treat them as private information of the client. Note that for the privacy concern, in any LBA updating interval, the charging events sent to the edge server are *randomly* sampled from each client's event DB. This ensures that only partial charging information would be uploaded, and thus a malicious attacker at the edge server cannot restore the complete LBA model of any specific client.

Remark 3.4 Although the local LBA model at the edge server is updated periodically, this does not bring any impact to our LPVS solution given in Sect. 3.5. Specifically, without making any other modifications, we only need to replace the original LBA model (i.e., $\phi(\cdot)$ in the objective function of (3.13)) with the newly updated one, at the end of each updating interval.

3.7 Implementations

3.7.1 Real-World Video Streaming Traces

We target the *live video streaming service*, as it becomes extremely popular in recent years. It is reported by *Twitch*, a popular live video streaming platform, that in 2017 only, 355 billion minutes of live streams were watched and more than 2 million streamers had broadcast channels on the platform [58]. We then use a dataset from *Twitch* as input requests for our evaluations.

The dataset consists of traces from thousands of live-streaming channels in 2014, with a sampling interval of 5 minutes. It includes detailed information, such as the number of viewers in each channel, bitrate of each channel, and duration of each channel. We filter the data and only keep the live channels that last for no more than 10 hours, which results in 1566 live channels and 4761 live video sessions. The histogram of video session durations is given in Fig. 3.6.

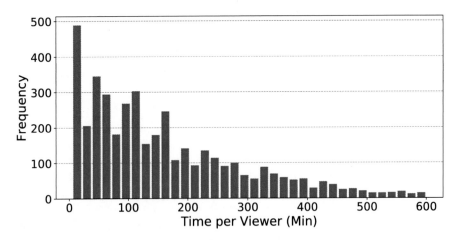

Fig. 3.6 The histogram of video session durations in our dataset

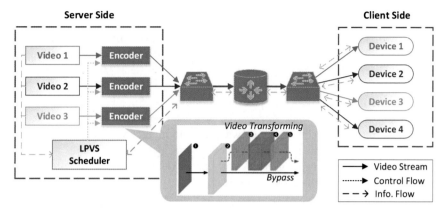

Fig. 3.7 The framework of LPVS emulator and its major building blocks

3.7.2 LPVS Emulation and Setups

To emulate the whole process of LPVS and validate its effectiveness, we develop an emulator with building blocks shown in Fig. 3.7. The major procedures include information gathering, request scheduling, and video transforming.

(1) Information Gathering

Rationale At each scheduling point of LPVS, along with their video (chunks) requests, the users (mobile devices) report the displays' information (e.g., size and resolution) as well as the energy status to the LPVS scheduler. Meanwhile, the video information (e.g., whether cached and currently available) is also collected from either the CDN PoP or edge streaming server. In addition, as introduced in Sect. 3.4.2, the power rates of requested videos (chunks) are also estimated at the server side, aided by existing power modeling and profiling techniques for LCD in [39] and OLED in [12], respectively.

Setups The scheduling period (i.e., length of the time slot) of LPVS is set to 5 minutes, which is consistent with the sampling interval of the *Twitch* dataset. A group of viewers in each channel of *Twitch* are selected and form a virtual cluster (VC) in our context. Some needed information to drive LPVS can be obtained from the dataset, e.g., the number of live channels/videos, the number of chunks in each time slot, and the resolutions of requested videos. For other information that cannot be learnt from the dataset, e.g., the power rate of live videos and the specifications of displays, we assign values for each of them by randomly choosing from available display resolutions under the supported bitrates. As to the energy status of the mobile devices, it is also not contained in the dataset, so we randomly assign values following a Gaussian distribution at the beginning of emulation.

(2) Request Scheduling

Rationale At the server side, for low-power video streaming, with the gathered information of user requests ($d_n(t)$ defined by (3.1)), display specifications (inputs of the resource consumption functions $g(\cdot)$ and $h(\cdot)$ in Sect. 3.4.4), energy status ($e_{n,m}(1)$), and video metadata (e.g., bitrates, power rates $p_{n,m}(\kappa)$), the LPVS scheduler performs the video request scheduling task. Specifically, by following the solution methodology introduced in Sect. 3.5, the scheduler is able to select the optimal subset of the requested videos for transforming, under the constraints of edge server capacity. This returns a scheduling strategy that results in the maximum display energy saving and user low-battery anxiety reduction simultaneously. Meanwhile, for local LBA model updating at the server side, as introduced in Sect. 3.6, the charging events are reported to the server from each client upon the request by every updating interval.

Setups The LPVS scheduler works under the "one-slot-ahead" scheduling mode, i.e., during current slot the LPVS makes decision for the incoming requests in the next time slot. Then, at the scheduling point of next time slot, the obtained decision will be executed, with which the selected videos are sent to the encoders. We also experiment on different values of λ to validate the effectiveness of LPVS w.r.t. balancing the power saving and anxiety reduction. Furthermore, for the experiments of LBA model updating, the updating interval is set to one hour (i.e., $\Delta_s = 60$ minutes), and the number of charging events for each sampling at a client end is set to 10 (i.e., $q = 10$).

(3) Video Transforming

Rationale As shown in Fig. 3.7, all the requested videos will go through the encoder component at the server side. Within the video encoder, the selected videos (chunks) by the scheduler will be transformed using the techniques introduced in Sect. 3.2.2, and meanwhile the un-selected videos will bypass the transforming function. After the video transforming, the power saving ratio γ_n can be updated following our strategy in Sect. 3.5.4.

Setups The amount of videos that can be transformed simultaneously depends on the capacity of edge streaming server. Referring to one commercial edge server model from Nokia (AirFrame Open Edge Server [34]) and resource consumption measurements of video transcoding [35], we estimate that one edge server can process video streaming (including transforming) for up to 100 mobile devices simultaneously. Moreover, at the beginning of the first time slot, we set the prior distribution of γ_n by a Gaussian distribution with $\mu = (0.13 + 0.49)/2 = 0.31$ (refer to the average upper/lower bounds given in Table 3.1) and $\sigma = 12$.

3.8 Performance Evaluations

In this section, we evaluate the performance of LPVS, under sufficient and insufficient edge capacity, respectively. Furthermore, we also investigate the impact of LPVS on the time per viewer, i.e., the time of individual viewers spending on watching videos. The LBA model update scheme is validated and the overhead of LPVS is also evaluated. The parameter settings for the experiments are given in Table 3.2.

3.8.1 LPVS with Sufficient Edge Resource

We first analyze the performance of LPVS under sufficient edge resource conditions. As mentioned in our implementations, we choose the edge server with capacity supporting up to 100 mobile users' video transforming simultaneously. Thus, we look into the performance of LPVS for those VCs with no more than 100 mobile users (with group size ranging from 50 to 100 specifically).

3.8.1.1 Energy Saving of Mobile Devices

The results on energy saving can be found in Fig. 3.8, where the bar chart (in blue color) shows the percentage of energy saving after applying LPVS. The average

Table 3.2 Parameter settings

Description	Settings
Scheduling slot	5 minutes
Scheduling mode	one-slot-ahead
regularization parameter λ	0, 0.1, 0.5
LBA model update interval Δ_s	60 minutes
# charging events per sampling q	10
Prior distribution for γ_n	$\mathcal{N}(0.31, 12)$

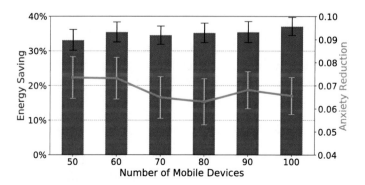

Fig. 3.8 Energy saving and anxiety reduction under sufficient edge resource

energy saving ratio of different testing groups is 35.20%, with the maximum energy saving ratio of 37.13%. Thus, it can be concluded that LPVS can save a large portion of energy of users' mobile devices.

3.8.1.2   Anxiety Reduction of Mobile Users

The results on users' anxiety alleviation can also be found in Fig. 3.8, with the orange line chart at the right Y-axis. Specifically, the percentages of user anxiety reduction after applying LPVS are given, under different user group sizes. The average anxiety reduction ratio of different testing groups is 6.82%, with the maximum anxiety reduction ratio of 7.36%. We can see that, with LPVS, the mobile users' anxiety can be alleviated, while the effect is not significant as that of energy saving. This is mainly caused by our experimental setup that the energy status follows a Gaussian distribution, which leads to the majority with an energy status around 50% where the anxiety curve is relatively flat (refer to Fig. 3.2). Nevertheless, as will be shown in Sect. 3.8.3, the impact of LPVS on the low-battery users is significant.

3.8.2   LPVS with Limited Edge Resource

We then look into the cases where the edge capacity is not enough, i.e., the computing and storage resources are insufficient to provide LPVS to all users but a selected subset. Specifically, we investigate the performance of LPVS in those VCs with user group sizes ranging from 100 to 500. In addition, since only a subset of users can be served with LPVS, the regularization parameter λ takes effect in balancing the energy saving and anxiety reduction.

3.8.2.1   Energy Saving of Mobile Devices

The energy saving ratios of multiple user groups are shown in Fig. 3.9a, under different settings of λ. We can see that, the energy saving ratio decreases with the increasing number of mobile users, as the portion of users that can take advantage of LPVS becomes smaller. In addition, with the increase of λ, the weight for energy saving in the objective (of problem (3.8)) becomes smaller, thus leading to the decrease of energy saving ratio in each VC group.

3.8.2.2   Anxiety Reduction of Mobile Users

The anxiety reduction ratios of mobile users under different VC groups are illustrated in Fig. 3.9b. Based on the results, the anxiety reduction ratio decreases

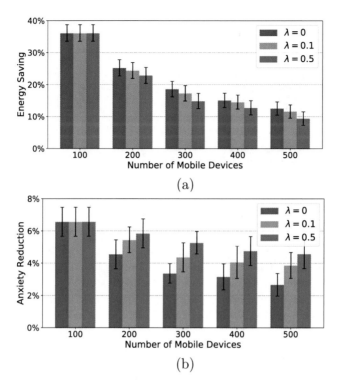

Fig. 3.9 Energy saving and anxiety reduction under the condition of limited edge server capacity. (**a**) Energy saving with LPVS under different values of λ. (**b**) Anxiety reduction with LPVS under different values of λ

with the increase of user group size, which is caused by the insufficient edge capacity. Furthermore, with the increase of λ, the weight for anxiety reduction in the objective function becomes larger, thus resulting in increased anxiety reduction for each VC group. It is also worth mentioning that we only illustrate the effectiveness of λ in balancing the energy saving and anxiety reduction. How to set the value of λ in practice is determined by the LPVS provider (based on specific policies and SLAs), which is beyond the scope of this work.

3.8.3 Impact of LPVS on Low-Battery Users

We have observed that the overall percentage in anxiety reduction with LPVS is not that obvious as that in energy saving, when the majority of users have relatively sufficient battery life. Nevertheless, when we shift our focus to the users who have low-battery status, the impact of LPVS is significant. To test the impact, we calculate the metric of time per viewer (TPV) for low-battery users, i.e., the time duration of

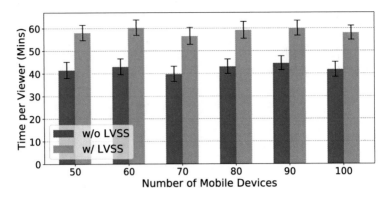

Fig. 3.10 Time per viewer increases with and without LPVS

individual users on video watching, under the sufficient edge capacity condition. The TPV metric is inferred from our online survey question: *At what battery level (in percentage from* 1 *to* 100%) *will you give up watching a video you are interested in on your mobile phone?*

For each VC group we have tested, we collect data on those users who were (1) selected for video transforming (served by LPVS) and (2) with energy status in (0, 40%] (so-called low-battery users) at the starting of LPVS. Then, we calculate the value of TPV for each low-battery user. For comparison, the TPV values without applying LPVS are also computed for these low-battery users.

The results are illustrated in Fig. 3.10 for the cases with and without applying LPVS, respectively. From the figure we can find that, without LPVS, the average value of TPV is 42.3 minutes, while with LPVS, the average TPV value increases to 58.7 minutes. This means that LPVS brings in an *extra* TPV of 16.4 minutes, which corresponds to 38.8% of the watching time duration of the low-battery users.

3.8.4   LPVS with Updated LBA Models

In this experiment, we first set a random monotonous decrease function f_{rnd} : $[0, 1] \rightarrow [0, 1]$ as the original *global* LBA model. The function is created by a four-step procedure: (1) divide the region of the independent variable into 100 bins, (2) sample a random number from the normal distribution for each of the bins, (3) create a cumulative histogram with the numbers of 100 bins, and (4) normalize the region of the dependent variable to [0, 1]. Then, we treat the LBA model extracted from our user survey as the "ground-truth"[4] *local* LBA model that the mobile users

---

[4] Here by "ground-truth" we mean that the LBA model captures the LBA features of mobile users appropriately in some way. It does not mean that the LBA model is the only one depicting the LBA features.

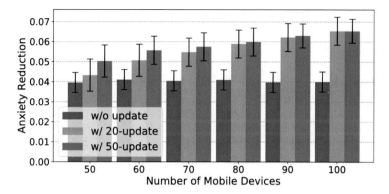

Fig. 3.11 The anxiety reduction from the LPVS solution, under updated LBA models (w/ 20-update and 50-update) and original LBA model (w/o update), respectively

adhere to, i.e., the users within the VC charge their phones following a cumulative distribution function in the shape of the LBA curve in Fig. 3.2.

Note that the above experiment design is to facilitate the evaluation of our LBA model updating method introduced in Sect. 3.6. Specifically, as we already have detailed data (on user charging behavior) for the local LBA model, the simulation for charging event sampling process becomes straightforward. In addition, for the experiment, we set the regularization parameter λ to a large value in this experiment, such that the influence of the power saving objective ($\psi_{n,m}(\kappa)$ in (3.8a)) could be neglected.

We update the original LBA model by following the procedure given in Sect. 3.6 and parameters set in Sect. 3.7.2-2 and look into the anxiety reduction performance from the LPVS solution. The results from 20 and 50 model updates, compared with that from the original model without any update, are shown in Fig. 3.11, respectively. From the results we can conclude that: (1) aided by the model updating scheme, the performance of anxiety reduction from LPVS can be much enhanced, by 38.6 and 45.4% for the 20-update and 50-update cases, respectively, and (2) along with the increase of updating iterations, the LBA model approaches the "ground-truth" gradually and achieve a steady (and the optimal) performance.

3.8.5   Overhead of LPVS and Impact on Other QoE Metrics

We treat LPVS as a value-added service upon the conventional video streaming and focus on evaluating the overhead of LPVS w.r.t. its running time. This is necessary when we adopt the "one-slot-ahead" working mode. If the scheduling cannot be finished in one time slot, it will affect the conventional video streaming service and may degrade other QoE metrics (e.g., increasing the video freezing time and frequency).

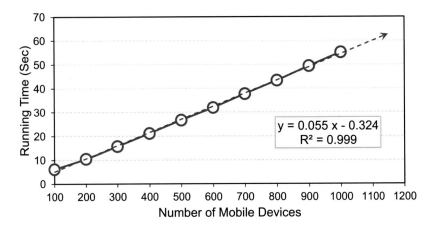

Fig. 3.12 Running times of LPVS scheduler with increase of VC group size; fitted by the linear regression function $y = 0.055x - 0.324$ with the R-squared value $R^2 = 0.999$

The average running time of LPVS resulting from our emulation is illustrated in Fig. 3.12, when performing optimal scheduling under different VC group sizes. We can observe that: (1) with the increase of user group size (i.e., number of mobile devices), the running time of LPVS increases accordingly; (2) the increasing trend is approximately linear, indicating the low time complexity of our heuristic method (given in Sect. 3.5.3). Under such a linear increase trend, the maximum number of mobile devices that our LPVS scheduler can handle is over five thousand, within the scheduling time slot of five minutes.

Note that we did not consider the overhead of video content transforming for this analysis, as it is actually completed in the (conventional) video encoding phase (refer to details of video transforming in Sect. 3.7.2). Therefore, the overhead of joint optimization for energy reduction and anxiety alleviation in LPVS can be well controlled following the "one-slot-ahead" working mode, thus making no impact on other QoE metrics (e.g., delay and jitter) of video streaming in practice. The perceptual impact of video transform has been well addressed (e.g., in [12]) and is beyond the scope of our work.

3.9 Conclusion

We presented LPVS for low-power video streaming services, which exploited an extracted (and periodically updated) LBA model for energy saving and LBA alleviation of mobile users. In specific, we modeled the problem of energy saving and anxiety reduction by a joint optimization problem at the edge server. Then, a two-phase heuristic method was developed to solve the problem. With an LPVS emulator and real-world trace data, we demonstrated that LPVS can save the overall mobile users' battery lives by up to 37% and prolong the low-battery users' video watching time by 39%.

The LBA model and empirical findings in this work could be applied in other applications, such as the quantification and alleviation of EV drivers' range anxiety. The major novelties of this work include (1) the LBA model extraction and update from user feedback or charging events, and (2) the application of the LBA model for energy saving and LBA reduction. Nevertheless, this work was limited to the situations at the mobile end and largely omitted the energy consumption of the edge server. We leave the exploration of energy saving potentials at the edge server as our future work.

Chapter 4
Optimal Backup Power Allocation for 5G Base Stations

4.1 Introduction

In the foreseeable future, 5G networks will be deployed rapidly around the world, in cope with the ever-increasing bandwidth demand in mobile network, emerging low-latency mobile services and potential billions of connections to IoT devices at the network edge [60]. As the first step shifting to the 5G era, the 5G base station (BS) needs to be built. With shorter signal range compared to that of 4G, the deployment of 5G network is expected to be highly dense. It is estimated that, by 2026 and in China only, over 14 million new and upgraded 5G BSs will be built, with 4.8 million macro BSs and another 9.5 million small ones [3].

With considerable power consumption of the 5G BS (2 ∼ 3 times of that of a 4G BS, referring to Fig. 4.2a), a large number of BS deployment means enormous communication power demands. These power demands, from one side, are satisfied by the power grid, and are safeguarded by backup batteries from the other side. As the power from the grid does not necessarily guarantee 100% uptime, the backup power provided by batteries is playing an important role. Due to lightning strikes, blown transformers, auto accidents, human theft and even rodents, power outages of BSs are actually much more than expected. Near one third of the BSs ever experienced power outages lasting for over 10 hours [61]. Therefore, BS power backup is in great need to keep the reliability of future mobile networks, especially for the macro BSs with large areas of network coverage and small ones

© The Author(s), under exclusive license to Springer Nature Singapore Pte Ltd. 2022
G. Tang et al., *GreenEdge: New Perspectives to Energy Management and Supply in Mobile Edge Computing*, SpringerBriefs in Computer Science,
https://doi.org/10.1007/978-981-16-9690-9_4

serving mission-critical mobile and edge services (e.g., connected and automated vehicles [62]).

Motivation and Opportunities To deploy backup batteries for BSs in 5G networks, however, demands a huge investment, especially considering that the Telecom revenue growth is slow [63]. Therefore, how to cut down the heavy cost of backup power while still ensuring the network reliability has become a critical and urgent problem. Replacing the traditional lead-acid batteries with lithium ones in power backup is one option and trend, as the latter uses more cost-efficient materials that is more reliable, efficient and space-saving [64]. In this work, from another side of battery deployment, we tackle the problem by providing the most cost-efficient allocation of backup power. Specifically, we explore possible opportunities for cost saving from both spatial and temporal dimensions.

4.1.1   Spatial Dimension

A naive solution is to equip each BS with an individual backup battery (group), while it is also the most expensive solution without taking any advantage of the BS deployment scenario. Considering the 5G heterogeneous network (HetNet) architecture with ultra dense small BS deployment, it is possible to share the backup power among multiple BSs. As illustrated in Fig. 4.1, one backup battery group can be shared among multiple small BSs (whose signal ranges are also covered by the nearby macro BS). Especially for the cloud radio access network (C-RAN) scenario with many baseband units (BBUs) pooled together, it is natural and convenient to supply backup power for those BSs all together.

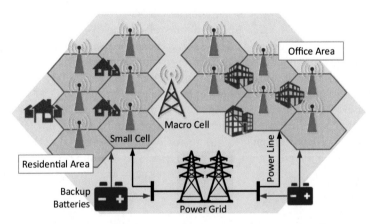

Fig. 4.1 The scenario of 5G HetNet consisting of macro and small cells, in which the backup power is supplied by battery groups. Ultra-dense small cells are deployed in the residential and office areas, where the amount of end users and their mobile data demands are large

4.1.2   Temporal Dimension

The time-varying traffic and power demands of BSs can also be exploited to further cut down the backup power cost. For example, with prior knowledge about the load patterns of small BSs within the coverage of a same macro cell, there are chances to shrink the maximum capacity of backup batteries to tightly meet the aggregated power demands. Similarly, for those small BSs deployed at different areas and showing particular patterns of traffic and power demands, it is also possible to perform strategic BS combinations for cost-efficient backup power sharing.

Previous solutions on backup power allocation of BSs were mostly targeted at 4G or older generation of networks. As the BSs in those networks are deployed sparsely, dedicated battery installation for individual BSs is the common practice. For example, as introduced in [61] and [65], the dedicated battery allocation was conducted and optimized to reduce the service interruption and deployment cost, based on the features of individual BSs. As large-scale 5G network deployment is around the corner, new solutions to cost-efficient backup power allocation for the ultra-dense BSs are in great need.

Contributions   Aiming at cost reduction, our idea is to share backup power among the ultra-dense BSs as much as possible, by seeking optimization opportunities from both spatial and temporal dimensions. Meanwhile, the backup power is strategically allocated under practical conditions, e.g. the probability of network failures should be less than a threshold. To achieve the above goals, we propose ShiftGuard and make the following contributions in this work.

- We investigate the real-world power consumption of 4G and 5G BSs and apply the observations and empirical findings to guide our design of backup power allocation.
- We model the optimal backup power allocation as a mixed-integer linear programming, where the multiplexing gain of BSs power demands is exploited and the network reliability is quantified with a backup power outage probability.
- With various experiments, we demonstrate that ShiftGuard can save the cost of backup power allocation by $27 \sim 40\%$, compared to the strategy without backup power sharing or simply sharing backup power with nearby BSs.

4.2   Related Work

A systematical analysis on a real-world dataset of BS backup battery groups was made in [66], in which the author also proposed a battery profiling method to find battery features that cause its degradation. Based on the feature profiling of BSs and their equipped battery groups, the author further formulated an optimization problem for battery allocation, aiming to minimize the service interruptions and deployment cost. Also, some real-world factors (e.g., the importance of different base stations, the available budget, etc.) were also taken into consideration [61, 65].

In the above relevant work, the author targeted at the BSs in 4G/LTE networks and the situation in next generation networks was not considered. It is well known that 5G BSs are much different from the 4G ones, including the deployment density, power consumption characters (refer to Sect. 4.3 for details) and so on. Thus, new strategies are needed to tackle the optimal backup power allocation problem in the upcoming 5G networks. Furthermore, previous backup power allocation strategies did not consider power sharing, most probably due to the spare deployment of BSs in their investigated networks. Our work is the first to propose backup power sharing among the dense (5G) BSs and take advantage of the statistical multiplexing gain to reduce the backup battery allocation cost.

4.3   BS Power Measurements and Observations

Collaborated with the mobile network operators, we were able to obtain the power consumption measurements of 4G and 5G BSs in the wild. Specifically, the power consumption of major components from four BSs were metered: (1) one 4G BS with average power readings of its major components of RRU (remote radio unit) and BBU, and (2) three 5G BSs with average power readings of their major components of AAU (active array unit) and BBU. Note that the AAU (for 5G BSs) is with similar functions to the RRU (for 4G BSs), and either 5G or 4G BSs has the component of BBU.

4.3.1   Power Consumption of 4G and 5G BSs

The power consumption comparison between the 4G and 5G BSs is shown in Fig. 4.2a, where we can observe that:

- the 5G BS consumes much more (about $2 \sim 3$ times) energy than that of the 4G BS, and the gap between them increases when the load rate (i.e., the ratio of specified mobile traffic amount to the maximum traffic load of BS is higher.
- Along with the increase of the load rate, the power consumptions of both 4G and 5G BSs increase accordingly, and the power growth of the 5G BS is faster than that of the 4G BS.

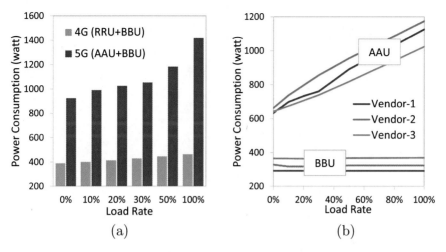

Fig. 4.2 Power measurements of the major components (AAU/RRU and BBU) at various load rate of four BSs, including one 4G BS and three 5G BSs. (**a**) Power cons. (4G vs. 5G). (**b**) Power cons. (5G AAU vs. BBU)

4.3.2 Power Consumption of 5G BS Major Components

The power consumption comparison of the major components (AAU and BBU) in 5G BSs is shown in Fig. 4.2b, from which we can observe that:

- the power consumption of the BS is dominated by the AAU component, as the AAU consumes much more (about $2 \sim 4$ times, depending on the vendor) energy than that of the BBU.
- the power consumption of AAU nearly linearly increases with the growth of BS load rate, while that of the BBU is quite stable at varying load rates.

As the power consumption of 5G BSs is significantly higher than that of 4G BSs, we focus on the backup power allocation of 5G networks in this work. Moreover, if the network adopts a C-RAN architecture where many BBUs are centralized, considering that the BBU is with stable power consumption and may be equipped with dedicated (backup) power supplies, we could also target at the AAUs of 5G BSs separately and allocate backup power for them accordingly.

4.3.3 Multiplexing Gain with Backup Power Sharing

According to the observations in Fig. 4.2b, we can estimate the power consumption of a 5G BS based on its traffic load. As the mobile data demands of end users within one area are time-varying across the day, the traffic load as well as the power demand of the nearby BSs fluctuates up and down accordingly. We have noticed that (1) the

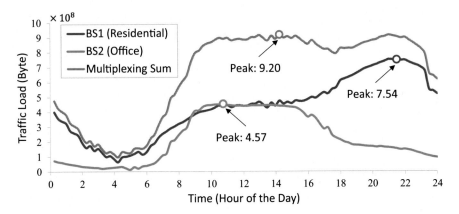

Fig. 4.3 Traffic load patterns of two real-world BSs in the residential area (blue curve) and office area (orange curve), respectively [67], along with their multiplexing sum (grey curve). The peak values of three curves are annotated

traffic load (or power demand) curves of the BSs at different areas usually follow different patterns determined by the user behaviour within the areas, and (2) most likely these traffic load (or power demand) curves would not reach their peak values at the same time.

As illustrated in Fig. 4.3, the power demand curves of one BS at the office area and another at the residential area are quite different. Specifically, the peak power demand of the BS at the office area appears in the daytime while the one at the residential area in the evening. The staggered peaks of two curves bring the so-called *statistical multiplexing gain*: the peak demand of their aggregation is most probably smaller than the sum of two separated peak values, as verified from Fig. 4.3. The aggregation of two curves (the grey curve in Fig. 4.3) is named *multiplexing sum* in this work.

Hence, when sharing backup power among multiple BSs, the statistical multiplexing gain can be exploited to reduce the capacity (thus the cost) of allocated backup batteries. Figure 4.4 gives a simple yet concrete example to show the benefit of multiplexing gain. In the example, two batteries are allocated to two BSs groups, namely *virtual cells* (VCs), with each VC containing three BSs and located in the residential or office area. In Strategy-I illustrated by Fig. 4.4a, with BSs in one area sharing the same battery, as they have similar power demand patterns and thus reach peak powers at the same time, we need to allocate 18 and 20 units of backup power for the two batteries respectively. In Strategy-II, by exchanging two BSs in the two VCs, as shown in Fig. 4.4b, the aggregated peak power demands of the BSs in the two VCs become different as the multiplex gain takes effect, resulting in only 10 units of backup power needed for each battery (~50% reduction of battery capacity cost).

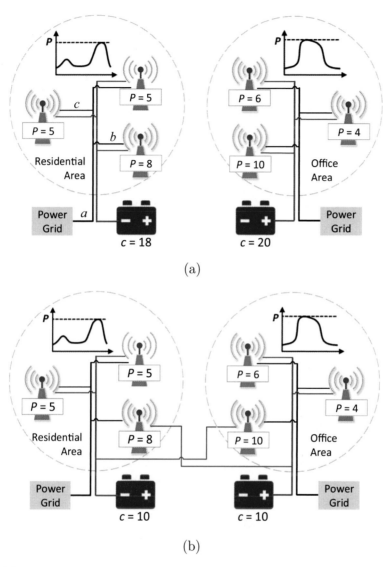

Fig. 4.4 Two backup power allocation strategies. Strategy II exploits the multiplexing gain of different power demand curves at the two areas, where P stands for peak power demand of the BS and c represents the allocated capacity of backup batteries. (**a**) Backup power allocation of two virtual cells (Strategy I). (**b**) Backup power allocation of two virtual cells (Strategy II)

4.4   System Model

In our scenario of backup power sharing and allocation, we mainly consider the small BSs that are densely deployed and account for the major proportion of 5G BSs. For the macro BSs, they are usually equipped with dedicated backup batteries and do not share backup power with others. However, by slightly modification, our system model for the scenario of small BSs can be compatible with that of macro BSs. Without specification, we use "BS" or "base station" in the later context to refer to "small base station".

4.4.1   Scenario Overview

4.4.1.1   Base Stations

Within the target area of 5G network, we assume that there are M BSs, with labels included in the set $\mathcal{U} = \{1, 2, \cdots, M\}$. The locations of all BSs are denoted by $\ell^{BS} = \{\ell_1^{BS}, \ell_2^{BS}, \cdots, \ell_M^{BS}\}$, with $\ell_m^{BS}, 1 \leq m \leq M$ denoting the location (e.g., latitude and longitude) of BS m.

4.4.1.2   Backup Batteries

In practice, the battery groups (either traditional lead-acid batteries or emerging lithium ones) are deployed as the backup power supply of BSs. In our scenario, one battery group could be shared by multiple BSs nearby to exploit the statistical multiplexing gain, and the multiple BSs sharing the same battery group form a *virtual cell* (VC). We name the candidate locations for potential battery deployment as *presence of points* (PoPs), and assume that there are N PoPs in the target network, with labels included in the set $\mathcal{V} = \{1, 2, \cdots, N\}$. Note that in our backup power sharing scenario, the number of BSs can be far bigger than that of PoPs, i.e., $N \ll M$. In addition, the locations of all PoPs can be represented by $\ell^{PoP} = \{\ell_1^{PoP}, \ell_2^{PoP}, \cdots, \ell_N^{PoP}\}$, with $\ell_n^{PoP}, 1 \leq n \leq N$ representing the location of PoP n.

4.4.1.3   Battery Capacity and Deployment

We define a *capacity vector*:

$$x := [x_1, x_2, \cdots, x_N]^\mathsf{T} \tag{4.1}$$

where x_n represents the capacity of battery group allocated at the n-th PoP (usually in unit of ampere·hour or AH). Then, we further define a *deployment indication matrix*:

$$y := \begin{bmatrix} y_{1,1} & y_{1,2} & \cdots & y_{1,M} \\ y_{2,1} & y_{2,2} & \cdots & y_{2,M} \\ \vdots & \vdots & \ddots & \vdots \\ y_{N,1} & y_{N,2} & \cdots & y_{N,M} \end{bmatrix} \tag{4.2}$$

in which $y_{n,m}$ is a binary value, with $y_{n,m} = 1$ denoting that (the battery at) PoP n supplies backup power to BS m and otherwise $y_{n,m} = 0$.

4.4.2   Traffic Load and Power Demand

For an interested time window, e.g., 6:00–12:00 AM, we evenly split the time into T consecutive slots, denoted by $\mathcal{W} = \{1, 2, \cdots, T\}$. For an arbitrary BS m, we define the inferred time-varying traffic load during the time window by a *load demand vector*:

$$d_m := [d_m(1), d_m(2), \cdots, d_m(T)]^\mathsf{T} \tag{4.3}$$

where $d_m(t)$ represents the load demand of BS m at time slot t, $1 \leq m \leq M$, $1 \leq t \leq T$. We assume that the load demand at each BS is periodic (e.g., with period of 24 hours) and with a relatively stable pattern. This assumption can be verified by the real-world traffic load data obtained from 9600 BSs in [67].

Then, the *power demand vector* is defined to denote the energy needed by the BS in each time slot:

$$e_m := [e_m(1), e_m(2), \cdots, e_m(T)]^\mathsf{T} \tag{4.4}$$

where $e_m(t)$ represents the estimated energy demand of BS m during time slot t. Referring to Sect. 4.3, $e_m(t)$ can be estimated by an empirical transformation function $f(d_m(t))$ from traffic loads to power demands, and we treat the transformation function $f(\cdot)$ as known domain knowledge. Then, we traverse the power demand vector of BS m and find the maximum element, i.e., the *peak power demand*, as:

$$P_m = \max_{t \in T} \{e_m(t)\}. \tag{4.5}$$

Remark 5 The load pattern at each BS can be obtained by (1) referring to its historical user traffic data, if the BS has already been installed for some while, or (2) learning from other similar BSs with the emerging techniques like *transfer learning* [68], if the BS is newly deployed.

4.5   Optimal Backup Power Allocation

4.5.1   Analysis of Power Outages and Network Failure

Given the backup power sharing scenario in Sect. 4.3.3 and illustrated by Fig. 4.4, two types of power outages may happen.

4.5.1.1 Synchronous Outage

Power outage occurs on the power line between power grid and a VC, e.g., line a in Fig. 4.4a is cut off. When such a power outage happens, it will cause all the BSs within the VC losing power at the same time, and we name such power outages of BSs *synchronous outages*. To deal with the synchronous outages, we allocate backup power according to the multiplexing sum of all BSs' power demands in the VC, by the constraint:

$$x_n \geq max\left\{\bigoplus_{m=1}^{M} e_m x_{n,m}\right\}, \forall n \in \mathcal{V} \tag{4.6}$$

where $\bigoplus$ represents the operation of statistical multiplexing (equivalent to vector addition), i.e., the allocated power capacity should be no less than the peak power of the multiplexing sum. Thus, when synchronous outages happen, the battery group can supply power to all BSs within the VC for a requirement time period (referred as *reserve time* and normally $10 \sim 12$ hours [65]).

4.5.1.2 Asynchronous Outage

Power outage occurs on the power line within the VC, e.g., line b and/or line c in Fig. 4.4a is cut off. When multiple such power outages happen, it means the failure of multiple BSs within the VC are at different time, and we name such power outages *asynchronous outages*. The battery group may not be able to satisfy the backup supply requirement, when asynchronous outages of many BSs happens with peak energy demands at different time. Taking the case in Fig. 4.4b as an example, the asynchronous outages: an outage of the BS in the office area in daytime peak hours and following another BS outage in the residential area in evening peak hours, can cause insufficient backup power supply and eventually lead to the network failure.

For a given set of BSs denoted by $\mathcal{Q} = \{q_1, q_2, \cdots, q_{|\mathcal{Q}|}\}$ with the number of BSs represented by $|\mathcal{Q}|$, the *synchronous peak power demand* of all BSs in this set is defined as the maximum of the multiplexing sum of all BSs' power demand curves, denoted by $S_{\mathcal{Q}}$, i.e.,

$$S_{\mathcal{Q}} = max\{\bigoplus_{q=1}^{|\mathcal{Q}|} e_q\} \tag{4.7}$$

where $\bigoplus$ represents the operation of statistical multiplexing. In contrast, the *asynchronous peak power demand* is defined as the sum of peak power demands of all BSs in this set, denoted by $A_{\mathcal{Q}}$, i.e.,

$$A_{\mathcal{Q}} = \sum_{i=1}^{|\mathcal{Q}|} P_{q_i} \tag{4.8}$$

Referring to Eq. (4.5) and Fig. 4.3, we can easily derive that $S_Q \leq A_Q$ (which also reflects the theoretical basis of our backup power sharing strategy).

For an arbitrary PoP n, we include the BSs within its associated VC in the set $\mathcal{U}_n$, with the number of BSs denoted by $|\mathcal{U}_n|$. Then, according to Eqs. (4.7) and (4.8), the synchronous and asynchronous peak power demands of the VC are $S_{\mathcal{U}_n}$ and $A_{\mathcal{U}_n}$, respectively. For any subset of $\mathcal{U}_n$ (denoted by $\mathcal{Z}$), we add it into a super set (denoted by $\mathcal{U}_n'$) if its asynchronous peak power demand is greater than the synchronous peak power demand of $\mathcal{U}_n$, i.e.,

$$\mathcal{U}_n' = \{\mathcal{Z} | \mathcal{Z} \subseteq \mathcal{U}_n \text{ and } A_{\mathcal{Z}} > S_{\mathcal{U}_n}\}. \tag{4.9}$$

Then, we find that only the BSs in any of the sets in $\mathcal{U}_n'$ can cause network failures by particular asynchronous outages.

4.5.2 Condition of Network Reliability

To keep the network reliability, we need to control the possibility of network failures caused by asynchronous outages under a predefined threshold (denoted by ϵ).

We look into an arbitrary set $\mathcal{Z} \in \mathcal{U}_n'$, with the elements of BSs labelled by $z_1, z_2, \cdots, z_{|\mathcal{Z}|}$ (note that $|\mathcal{Z}| \leq |\mathcal{U}_n|$). For any of the BS in $\mathcal{Z}$, say z_j, we first compute its *average power outage times* (λ_{z_j}) in the interested time window $\mathcal{W}$, e.g., by simply leveraging the total number of historical outages during a certain time period:

$$\lambda_{z_j} = \frac{\#\text{power outages}}{\#\text{corresponding time slots}} \cdot |\mathcal{W}| \tag{4.10}$$

Then the probability of network failure caused by BSs in $\mathcal{Z}$ over a time period with length of $q \cdot |\mathcal{W}|$ (where q is an integer and $q \geq 1$) can be approximately estimated by:

$$\Pr(\mathcal{Z}) = \binom{q}{1} \cdot \prod_{j=1}^{|\mathcal{Z}|} \lambda_{z_j} \tag{4.11}$$

where $\binom{q}{1}$ stands for choosing 1 from q.

Therefore, with the probability threshold of network failure ϵ, the following condition needs to be held:

$$\Pr(\mathcal{Z}) \leq \epsilon, \forall \mathcal{Z} \subseteq \mathcal{U}_n', \forall n \in \mathcal{V} \tag{4.12}$$

4.5.3   Backup Power Deployment Constraints

Further practical constraints during the backup power deployment are as follows.

- **No BS misses**: for any BS, its backup power is supplied by the batteries at one PoP (multiple PoPs backup supplying one BS is not considered):

$$\sum_{n=1}^{N} y_{n,m} = 1, \forall m \in \mathcal{U}. \tag{4.13}$$

- **Max battery capacity**: for any PoP, the maximum capacity of backup batteries that can be allocated is set as C. Then we have:

$$x_n \leq C, \forall n \in \mathcal{V}. \tag{4.14}$$

- **Max power line length**: due to energy loss and voltage drop in electricity transmission, the allowed maximum length of the power lines deployed within each VC (for each PoP) is set as L. Thus, we have:

$$\sum_{m=1}^{M} y_{n,m} \| \ell_m^{BS} - \ell_n^{PoP} \|_2 \leq L, \forall n \in \mathcal{V}. \tag{4.15}$$

4.5.4   Backup Power Allocation Optimization

Note that among the above mathematical representations, only x and y are unknown variables that need to solve, and all the other nations are either prior knowledge or known parameters.

Given the above assumptions and conditions, the following optimization problem can be formulated to minimize the allocated backup power capacity (thus minimize the backup power cost):

$$\min_{\{x,y\}} \quad \sum_{n=1}^{N} x_n \tag{4.16a}$$

$$\text{s.t.} \quad (4.6), (4.9), (4.12) \sim (4.15). \tag{4.16b}$$

The above problem belongs to the mixed-integer linear programming (MILP) which could be intractable when the problem scale is large. Fortunately, considering the energy loss and voltage drop along the power line, the number of BSs that a battery group can connect to and support cannot be large (e.g., several dozens). Thus, with some off-the-shelf MILP solvers, we are able to tackle the optimization problem efficiently. For example, in our experiments of backup power allocation among 100 BSs, PuLP [69] with a CBC solver could help us find the optimal solution normally within 1 minute on a low-end desktop.

4.6 Experimental Evaluations

4.6.1 Experiment Setup

4.6.1.1 Scenario

We consider a distributed backup power allocation scenario, where multiple small BSs are deployed in one macro cell and the BSs within the same macro cell are considered together for backup power allocation. In our simulations, 100 small BSs are deployed within one macro cell (a $1 \times 1\,$km square). Then, PoP candidates are configured as potential points for backup power allocation, and the number of PoPs are randomly set to $8 \sim 25$ in one macro cell.

4.6.1.2 BS Power Demands

The power demand of each BS is referred to the cases given in Fig. 4.3, i.e., the traffic demand of residential or office area is simulated at each BS. To be realistic, we first partition the whole targeted area into small subareas and configure the BSs in each subarea with only one type of traffic/power demand. For example, as illustrated in Fig. 4.7, four subareas with two residential subareas and two office subareas are considered as a case study.

4.6.1.3 Benchmarks

We compare our ShiftGuard with two benchmarks: (1) NoShare strategy, which simply allocates individual BS with backup power equal to its peak demand and without any sharing; (2) SimpleShare strategy, which shares backup power with those BSs nearest the PoPs and thus yields the shortest power line usage within each VC.

4.6.2 Results and Analysis

4.6.2.1 Cost Saving vs. Number of PoPs

Compared with the two benchmarks, we look into the total capacity allocated at all PoPs, as this metric directly reflects the cost saving in backup power allocation.

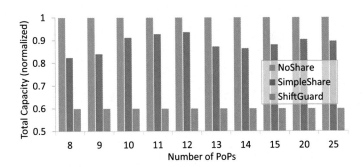

Fig. 4.5 The (normalized) total capacity resulted from three different strategies under different number of PoPs. Parameter setting: #BS = 100, $C = 1000$, $L = 1000$

Base on the results shown in Fig. 4.5, we can see that, with different number of PoPs, **ShiftGuard** always results the least total capacity of allocated backup power, with a cost saving of 40% against the **NoShare** benchmark and $27 \sim 36\%$ againest the **SimpleShare** benchmark.

4.6.2.2   Cost Saving vs. C and L

We then regulate two important parameters: the battery group capacity at each PoP C and the maximum allowed power line length L. With different settings of C and L, we get the results in Fig. 4.6, from which we can conclude that: compared with the two benchmarks, **ShiftGuard** always yields the least total capacity (thus the least cost) and would perform better when C or L gets larger.

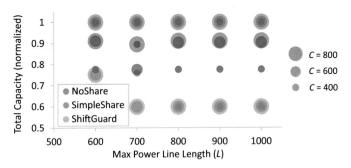

Fig. 4.6 The (normalized) total capacity resulted from three different strategies under different settings of battery group capacities and maximum allowed power line lengths. Other parameter setting: #BS = 100, #PoP = 10

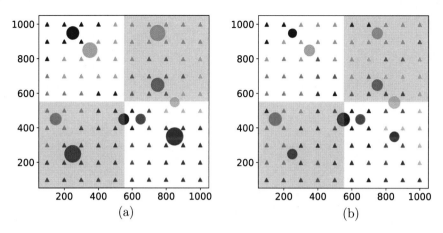

Fig. 4.7 Case study of (**a**) SimpleShare and (**b**) ShiftGuard within one macro cell. The two shaded areas are residential subareas and the other two are office subareas. Triangles represents the BSs and bubbles are the PoP locations. The color of BSs and PoPs shows which VC they belong to, and the size of bubble indicates resulted battery capacity from corresponding strategy

4.6.2.3 Case Study

To specifically compare ShiftGuard and SimpleShare benchmark, we look into one detailed case and corresponding results, shown in Fig. 4.7. From the colored triangles (BSs) and sized bubbles (PoPs) illustrated in the figure, we are able to distinguish the allocation differences of the two strategies and figure out why ShiftGuard performs better: within the allowed power line length, ShiftGuard takes advantage of the multiplexing gain by supplying backup power to BSs in different areas, while SimpleShare simply supplies backup power to BSs nearest each PoP.

4.7 Conclusion

In this chapter, we proposed an optimal backup power allocation framework for BSs, ShiftGuard, to help the mobile network operators reduce their backup power cost in shifting to the 5G network and beyond. We modeled the problem as an MILP to minimize the allocated backup battery capacity, considering the network reliability and other practical constraints in backup battery deployment. The results from various experiments validated the superiority of ShiftGuard, compared with the strategy without backup power sharing or simply sharing with nearby BSs.

Chapter 5
Reusing Backup Batteries for Power Demand Reshaping in 5G

5.1 Introduction

To cope with the ever-increasing demands of mobile broadband, low-latency communications and IoT connections in the future wireless network, the worldwide mobile network operators are upgrading their network facilities and marching towards the 5G network at an unprecedented pace. Compared with the older generation networks like 4G/LTE, the signal range of a 5G base station (BS) is much shorter, resulting in the ultra-dense BS deployment (also know as *network densification* [71]), especially for fully signal coverage in the urban or "hotspot" areas. According to [3], by 2026 and in China only, over 14 million 5G BSs will be built.

To deploy and operate such a large-scale BSs, however, it needs an enormous investment, covering both capital expense (CAPEX) and operating expense (OPEX). The OPEX, in particular, is mainly attributed to the electricity consumed by the BSs. It has been well noticed that the newly constructed 5G BSs are with considerable power consumption. According to the power metering results from the mobile operators, as illustrated in Fig. 4.2, the power consumption of a 5G BS is typically 2~3 times of that of a 4G BS. Considering the large-scale and ultra-dense deployment of 5G BSs in the near future, it could lead up to a tenfold increased electricity cost [6]. Consequently, the energy consumption of BSs could become a huge burden of the mobile operators, and how to cut down the energy cost is among the top priorities with the shift to 5G and beyond.

© The Author(s), under exclusive license to Springer Nature Singapore Pte Ltd. 2022   67
G. Tang et al., *GreenEdge: New Perspectives to Energy Management and Supply in Mobile Edge Computing*, SpringerBriefs in Computer Science,
https://doi.org/10.1007/978-981-16-9690-9_5

The energy cost of the mobile operator is typically composed by (1) *energy charge* that is based on the total consumed electricity amount (in kWh) and (2) *demand charge* which is determined by the peak power demand (in kW) as a penalty. Particularly, the demand charge from severe unbalanced power consumption could account for a large proportion of the electricity bill, e.g., it could be up to 8x the energy charge for a commercial datacenter in Georgia, US [72]. As a result for the mobile operators, if they can cut down the demand charges, they can lower the energy cost accordingly, given that the total amount of consumed energy is constant. In the current cellular network, however, there seems no way to flatten the peak power demands, e.g., by peak power shaving strategy of workload shifting [73], as the real-time traffic demands from mobile users can hardly be shifted or even delayed.

Observations and Opportunities When constructing a new BS, a backup battery with certain power capacity is usually deployed in accompaniment. It helps safeguard the BS's normal functioning against power outages for a reserved time (several to a dozen hours), as the power grid does not guarantee a 100% uptime. The backup batteries are necessary for nowadays BSs [61], especially those core and mission-critical BSs (e.g., colocating edge servers in mobile edge computing [62, 74]). Although a large-number of backup batteries have been or are going to be deployed, they are rarely used but lie idle in practice, especially in the urban areas where the grid power is ultra-stable.

To improve their utilization and cost efficiency, the backup batteries can be leveraged as natural candidates participating in the electricity regulation markets. Particularly, the backup battery can be transformed to and treated as a battery energy storage system (BESS). Then the distributed BESS can be utilized for BS power demand reshaping, e.g., discharging during the peak hours and recharging during the off-peak hours, and thus reduce the demand charges for the mobile operators. Meanwhile, the BESS's original duty of BS power backup can be barely affected.

Ideas and Challenges Aiming at demand charge reduction, we exploit the potential benefits of operating the backup batteries as a distributed BESS for peak power demand shaving. Ideally, with strategic battery discharge/charge scheduling, the power demands of BSs could be reshaped and flattened as much as possible, and the incurred demand charge of the network system could thus be minimized.

To realize the above goals, however, we are faced with several challenges. Firstly, it is not straightforward to model the optimal battery discharge/charge scheduling problem in a distributed manner, especially considering the spatial-temporal varying power demands of all BSs in the network system. Secondly, as the lifetime of a battery is limited and shortened along with discharge/charge cycles, how to quantify the battery's degradation/replacement cost and balance it with the demand charge saving are critical and challenging. Furthermore, as the BESS's discharge/charge operations should obey certain physical laws (e.g., discharge/charge rates are limited) and are bounded by realistic constraints (e.g., high depth of discharge is prohibited), how to incorporate these factors with the BESS operating problem is non-trivial.

Contributions By addressing the above challenges, we make the following contributions in this work.

- Based on the heterogeneous network (HetNet) architecture and distributed BESS scenario, we model the BESS discharge/charge scheduling as an optimization problem, which takes into account the practical considerations of BS power supply/demand as well as the backup battery specifications.
- After analysing the computational complexity of the optimization problem, we propose a deep reinforcement learning (DRL) based approach to solve the BESS discharge/charge scheduling problem. The DRL-based BESS scheduling approach accommodates all factors considered in the modeling phase and can adapt to the dynamic power demands from the BSs.
- Using a real-world BS deployment scenario and BS traffic load traces, we demonstrate that, leveraging the distributed BESS and our DRL-based scheduling approach, the demand charge of the mobile operator could be reduced by up to 26.59%, and corresponding yearly OPEX saving for 2282 5G BSs could reach US$185,000.

5.2 System Models

In this section, we present the system models applied and basic assumptions in this work.

5.2.1 Scenario Overview

As illustrated in Fig. 4.1, we consider the HetNet architecture for the future 5G network and beyond, where the macro BSs are deployed sparsely and mainly in charge of signal coverage in large-scale and the small BSs are densely deployed in the places where the mobile traffic demands are large, such as the residential and office areas. As the backup power of BSs, the backup battery[1] is equipped, either dedicated to one BS (e.g., the mission-critical and core BSs) or shared by multiple BSs (e.g., the densely deployed small BSs).

Given a targeted wireless network (5G or beyond), we assume that a number of M 5G BSs have been or are planning to be deployed. All the BSs can be denoted by a set $\mathcal{U} = \{1, 2, \cdots, M\}$. In the target network, we name the places where batteries

---

[1] A backup battery typically consists of multiple battery cells, thus also known as a battery group. We use the word "battery" for simplicity.

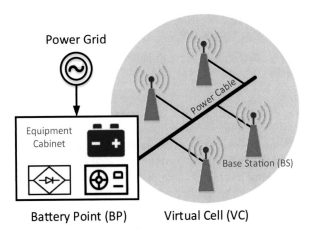

Fig. 5.1 Implementation of power supply and backup of a VC (containing four BSs) at a BP. The BP here is exemplified by an equipment cabinet, containing the rectifier (bottom-left of cabinet), power supply (bottom-right of cabinet) and backup battery (top-right of cabinet)

are deployed as *battery points* (BPs). In practice, there exist natural BP candidates for backup battery deployments, such as the BS equipment cabinets/rooms (shown in Fig. 5.1) or the telecom central offices. Assume that the number of BPs is N and they are denoted by the set $\mathcal{V} = \{1, 2, \cdots, N\}$. As one battery can be potentially shared by multiple BSs, we have $N \leq M$ under our scenario.

5.2.2   BS Power Supply and Demand

As shown in Fig. 5.1, the power of BSs is directly supplied by the power grid and backuped by the battery. The backup battery can be installed at any BP, with a certain capacity, and dedicated to one BS or shared by multiple BSs nearby [59]. Particularly, those BSs sharing the same backup battery form a *virtual cell* (VC), as illustrated by Fig. 5.1.

The battery capacity of each BP, referring to how fast and how much the BP can supply backup power to the BSs, is allocated based on the peak power demand of BSs within the associated VC. Particularly, to denote the battery capacity allocated at each BP, we define a *capacity vector* as follow:

$$c := [c_1, c_2, \cdots, c_N]^\mathsf{T} \tag{5.1}$$

in which c_n denotes the capacity of battery deployed at the n-th BP, typically in unit of ampere·hour or AH.

We consider a discrete time model, where the electricity billing cycle (e.g., one month) is evenly split into T consecutive slots with length of Δt and denoted by

$\mathcal{W} = \{1, 2, \cdots, T\}$. Thus, at an arbitrary BP n, the power demand of associated BSs during the billing cycle can be defined by a *power demand vector*:

$$p_n := [p_n(1), p_n(2), \cdots, p_n(T)]^\mathsf{T} \tag{5.2}$$

where $p_n(t)$ is the power demand at BP n in time slot t. Note that the power demands can be obtained by power meter readings at each BP. Alternatively, referring to Fig. 4.2b, the linear relationship between the traffic load and power consumption can be leveraged to estimate the power demands.

5.2.3   Battery Specification

At an arbitrary time slot t, we model the state of battery at BP n with a tuple:

$$\pi_n(t) := \langle SoH_n(t), SoC_n(t), DoD_n(t) \rangle \tag{5.3}$$

where the notations of SoH, SoC and DoD represent the *state of health*, *state of charge*, and *depth of discharge* of the battery, respectively. To be detailed: (1) **SoH** indicates the health condition of the battery, by quantifying the battery's actual lifetime over time, as a percentage of a new battery's capability, (2) **SoC** gives how much energy the battery currently stores, as a percentage of its capacity, and (3) **DoD** indicates how much energy the battery has released, as a percentage of its capacity. Notice that SoC is actually the complement of DoD. We adopt both metrics by following the common practice in BESS modeling, which also makes later descriptions more clear.

For simplicity, we discretize the SoC of a battery into K equal-spaced states, e.g., ten SoCs states of $\{10, 20, \cdots, 100\%\}$. Among the discrete SoC states, we use SoC_{min} and SoC_{max} to indicate the minimum and maximum SoCs for the battery's discharging and recharging, respectively. Note that the minimum and maximum SoCs are recommended by the vendor and prevent the battery from over-discharging/charging.

5.3   Power Demand Reshaping via BESS Scheduling

The backup batteries deployed at the BSs can be regarded as a distributed BESS. By discharging during the peak power time and recharging during the off-peak power time, it is able to reshape the total power demands of BSs and reduce the demand charge of the energy cost.

To represent the battery discharge/charge schedule, we define the *backup power supply vector* for the battery at BP n:

$$b_n := [b_n(1), b_n(2), \cdots, b_n(T)]^\mathsf{T} \tag{5.4}$$

where $b_n(t)$ is a real number variable and can be (1) **positive**: denoting the discharging power from the battery (instead of power grid) at BP n to the BSs during time slot t, (2) **negative**: indicating the charging power from the grid to the battery, or (3) **zero**: indicating that no discharging or charging happens.

5.3.1 Energy Cost with BESS

To quantify the energy cost (including energy charge and demand charge) of the targeted network system with BESS, we first assume the following electricity billing policy, which was widely applied in previous literature [72, 73, 75].

- Energy Charge: the total amount of consumed energy (in unit of kWh) of the network system multiplies the energy price (in unit of US$/kWh and denoted by λ_e).
- Demand Charge: the maximum power consumption (in unit of kW) of the network system during the billing cycle multiplies the peak power price (in unit of US$/kW and denoted by λ_d).

With the above billing policy, we then derive the energy charge and demand charge of the whole system (i.e., the targeted network system with BESS) for each time slot.

Given the power demands at each BP, $p_n(t)$, and the battery discharge/charge schedule, $b_n(t)$, we can formulate the *aggregated* power demand of the whole system for an arbitrary time slot t by:

$$A_{1:N}(t) = \sum_{n=1}^{N} \left(p_n(t) - \tilde{b}_n(t) \right) \tag{5.5}$$

where $\tilde{b}_n(t)$ is defined by:

$$\tilde{b}_n(t) = \begin{cases} \alpha \cdot b_n(t) \,, & \text{if } b_n(t) > 0 \\ b_n(t)/\beta \,, & \text{if } b_n(t) \le 0 \end{cases} \tag{5.6}$$

and represents the *net power* released/recharged from/to the battery considering the power loss in AC-DC conversion and battery leakage, with $\alpha \in (0, 1)$ and $\beta \in (0, 1)$ denoting the discharging and charging efficiencies, respectively.

Then, the incurred **energy charge** of the whole system during time slot t can be represented by:

$$\mathcal{J}^e(t) = \lambda_e A_{1:N}(t) \Delta t. \tag{5.7}$$

And according to the billing policy, the incurred **demand charge** (for aggregated peak power demand) in time slot t can be represented by:

$$\mathcal{J}^d(t) = \max\left\{0, \lambda_d\left(A_{1:N}(t) - A_{1:N}^{peak}\right)\right\} \tag{5.8}$$

where $A_{1:N}^{peak}$ records the peak power demand of the whole system during the past $t-1$ time slots. After the time slot t, if $A_{1:N}(t) > A_{1:N}^{peak}$ (or $\mathcal{J}^d(t) > 0$), $A_{1:N}^{peak}$ will be updated to $A_{1:N}(t)$.

5.3.2 Battery Degradation Cost

Every cycle of discharge/charge does some "harm" to the battery and reduces its lifetime. The battery has to be replaced by a new one when its SoH drops down to a preset "dead" level, denoted by SoH_{dead} in this work. In other words, there is an attached *degradation cost* for the battery with each discharge/charge cycle.

For any battery, we also know that it has a limited number of discharge/charge cycles, mainly determined by its chemical material (e.g., LA or LI) and usage pattern (e.g., DoD in each cycle). Thus, given the relationship between the DoD level and corresponding number of discharge/charge cycles, as illustrated in Fig. 5.5a, we are able to evaluate the degradation cost for each specific discharge event.

Given the state of battery at BP n after time slot $t-1$, i.e., $\langle SoH_n(t-1), SoC_n(t-1), DoD_n(t-1)\rangle$, the SoH decrease of the battery during this time slot can be measured by:

$$\Delta SoH_n(t) = \begin{cases} \frac{1-SoH_{dead}}{h(DoD_n(t-1)+\Delta DoD_n(t))} & , \text{if } b_n(t) > 0 \\ 0 & , \text{if } b_n(t) \leq 0 \end{cases} \tag{5.9}$$

where $h(\cdot)$ gives the total number of discharge/charge cycles that a battery can endure in its lifetime under an input DoD level (exemplified in Fig. 5.5a), and $\Delta DoD_n(t)$ gives the increase of DoD and can be calculated by:

$$\Delta DoD_n(t) = \frac{b_n(t)\Delta t}{c_n}. \tag{5.10}$$

With Eq. (5.9), we attribute the accumulated SoH decrease over the charge/discharge cycle into each time slot of discharging.

With the above expression of SoH decrease at each BP, we can then formulate the **degradation cost** of the distributed BESS for any arbitrary time slot t:

$$J^b(t) = \lambda_b \sum_{n=1}^{N} \Delta SoH_n(t) \tag{5.11}$$

in which λ_b is a coefficient converting the battery degradation to a monetary cost, with the unit of "US\$/SoH decrease".

5.3.3 Optimal BESS Operation Scheduling

5.3.3.1 Discharge/Charge Rate Constraint

The maximum charging rate of the battery at a BP, denoted by R^+, gives the largest power that the battery can be recharged with during a time slot. The maximum discharging rate of the battery can be denoted by R^-, which shows the largest power that the battery can supply with in a time slot. Thus, the following constraint holds:

$$-R^+ \leq b_n(t) \leq R^- \tag{5.12}$$

and according to [76], R^- is usually 5~10 times larger than R^+ for LA batteries.

5.3.3.2 SoC Constraint

For any arbitrary time slot, the SoC of battery at each BP is expected to follow the constraint:

$$SoC_{min} \leq SoC_n(t) \leq SoC_{max} \tag{5.13}$$

where SoC_{min} and SoC_{max} are the specified minimum and maximum SoCs, respectively. Particularly, to safeguard the BP against potential power outages, SoC_{min} should be set following the required reserved time of the backup battery.

5.3.3.3 Battery State Updating

Given the battery state of BP n at time $t-1$, i.e., $\pi_n(t-1)$, the battery state at time t can be updated by:

$$\pi_n(t) \leftarrow \begin{cases} SoH_n(t) = SoH_n(t-1) - \Delta SoH_n(t) \\ SoC_n(t) = SoC_n(t-1) - \Delta DoD_n(t) \\ DoD_n(t) = DoD_n(t-1) + \Delta DoD_n(t) \end{cases} \tag{5.14}$$

where $\Delta SoH_n(t)$ and $\Delta DoD_n(t)$ are given by Eqs. (5.9) and (5.10), respectively, and $SoC_n(0)$, $SoH_n(0)$ and $DoD_n(0)$ are the initial SoC, SoH and DoD of the battery, respectively.

For the billing cycle window $\mathcal{W}$, the following optimization problem can be formulated to find the optimal discharge/charge schedule for the distributed BESS.

$$\min_{b_n(t)} \quad \sum_{t=1}^{T} \left(\mathcal{J}^e(t) + \mathcal{J}^d(t) + \mathcal{J}^b(t) \right) \tag{5.15a}$$

$$\text{s.t.} \quad (5.12) \sim (5.14), \forall n \in \mathcal{V}, \forall t \in \mathcal{W}. \tag{5.15b}$$

5.3.4 Problem Analysis

Dynamic programming (DP) has been applied to solve the battery discharge/charge scheduling problem for long [77, 78]. The main idea of the DP approach is to evaluate all possible discharging/charging sequences of the battery step by step and wrap up the optimal sequence by backward tracing. For example, as illustrated by one slice (for one battery case) in Fig. 5.2, given the initial state of a battery, all paths (costs) from current state to possible states at next time are calculated, from

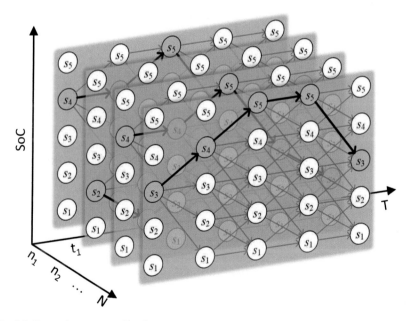

Fig. 5.2 Dynamic programming for discharge/charge scheduling of four batteries. One slice represents the scheduling process for one battery

which the least cost path will be recorded. The above process goes on until the end of the billing cycle. The optimal path is then traced backwards from the last state, after all possible paths have been traversed. When applying the above DP approach for distributed BESS operating in our case, however, we have two major challenges.

5.3.4.1 High Computational Complexity

The computational complexity in our case is way higher than that of the conventional one. First, the number of batteries increases from one to hundreds or even thousands in our set scenario (as shown in Fig. 5.4). Given such a large-scale distributed BESS, its discharge/charge scheduling is much more complex than one battery case as given in [77, 78]. Second, the time window considered in our work is much longer than the aforementioned work. Although with the same time slot length (15-min), previous work designed the DP approach for a one-day scheduling, while we consider the real-world billing cycle of one-month. Such a (30x) time length extension results in a considerable complexity increase. The above two changes lead to a much larger searching space, compared with the one battery scheduling case, and thus prohibit any brute-force based searching approach for the optimal solution, including the DP approach introduced above. As a direct measurement, the complexity for the one-day scheduling of one battery is $\mathcal{O}(TK^2)$, where T is the number of time slots in one-day and K is the number of possible SoC changes for a battery. Nevertheless, the complexity in our case increases to $\mathcal{O}(T'K^2N)$, where $T'(\gg T)$ is the number of time slots in one-month billing cycle and N is the number of BPs among the whole network system.

5.3.4.2 Dynamic Power Demand

Another major defect of applying DP approach in our case is that, it assumes that the power demands are known in advance and searches for the optimal schedule in an offline way [77, 78]. This assumption is too strong for our problem, as the traffic demands of BSs as well as their power demands are indeed dynamic and cannot be obtained beforehand. Although there are works for traffic demands forecasting in wireless network [67, 79], the results are usually rough patterns and cannot be quite precise. As a consequence, the conventional DP approach for offline scheduling optimization is unable to be applied for our problem. A new approach to BESS scheduling, which can deal with the dynamic power demands and make (discharge/charge) decisions in real-time, is in great need.

Lyapunov stochastic optimization was applied for online operating of energy storage [80, 81], whereas it could not guarantee satisfactory outcomes for small and medium sized energy storage [82] nor be directly applied in a distributed manner as in our case. To tackle the above challenges, we propose an online discharge/charge scheduling approach based on deep reinforcement learning in the following section.

5.4 A DRL-Based Approach to Distributed BESS Scheduling

The constantly changing power demands of distributed BSs makes it hard to yield optimal BESS scheduling for model-based strategies, whereas it gives the opportunity to the learning-based methods. In this section, we present an online discharge/charge scheduling approach based on deep reinforcement learning (DRL), which exploits past experiences (e.g., historical BS power demands) for better decision-making by adapting to current state of environment (e.g., real-time BS power demands and BESS SoCs).

5.4.1 DRL Based BESS Scheduling: Components and Concepts

A typical DRL framework consists of five key components: *agent*, *state*, *action*, *reward* and *policy*. Each component in our DRL-based BESS scheduling model is explained as follows.

- **Agent**: The role of the agent in BESS scheduling is to make decisions by inter-acting with the environment. Specifically, in our problem the agent determines the discharge/charge power at each BP in each time slot, according to the current states of power demand at each BS and SoC at each battery. The goal of the agent is to shave the peak power demand of the targeted network system, so as to minimize the total energy cost.
- **State**: The agent will be given a feedback state from the environment (i.e., the whole system) after taking a specific action. Specifically, at each time slot t, the state of the environment can be defined by a vector $s(t) = [A_{1:N}^{peak}, s_1(t), s_2(t), \ldots, s_N(t)]$, where $A_{1:N}^{peak}$ is the aggregated peak power demand in historical time slots and $s_n(t)(1 \leq n \leq N)$ is the state of VC at BP n and represented by $s_n(t) = \langle p_n(t), \pi_n(t) \rangle$.
- **Action**: The agent will take an action after observing the state of the environment. In our problem, the choice of action is a scheduling policy that indicates (1) whether the battery should be charged or discharged and (2) how much energy should be charged or released during each time slot. Therefore, the action taken at time t, denoted by $a(t)$, is equivalent to b_n defined in Eq. (5.4). Notably the action space of agent is discretized according to the battery's discrete SoC states and restricted by the preset constraints of Eqs. (5.12) $\sim$ (5.14).
- **Policy**: The policy is defined by $\phi: \mathcal{S} \to \mathcal{A}$, where $\mathcal{S}$ and $\mathcal{A}$ represent the state and action spaces, respectively. Thus, the policy gives the mapping from environment states to specific actions. By $a(t) = \phi(s(t))$, it indicates the action to be taken at time t under the state $s(t)$. In our problem, we generate the policy by training a neural network during interacting with the environment.

- **Reward**: The agent takes an action at an arbitrary time t, $a(t)$, after observing the environment state $s(t)$. Then at the next time slot $t + 1$, the agent will receive a reward from a reward function taking $a(t)$ and $s(t)$ as inputs. Thus the reward function is used to evaluate the effectiveness of the actions.

5.4.2 Reward Function Design

For an arbitrary time slot t, the agent first collects the state of the environment $s(t)$ and then takes action $a(t)$ accordingly. To evaluate the performance of action $a(t)$, we define the following reward function:

$$R(t) = V^e(t) + V^d(t) + V^b(t) \qquad (5.16)$$

in which:

- $V^e(t) = -\mathcal{J}^e(t)$, measures the action reward of battery discharge/charge to the energy charge at time slot t;
- $V^d(t) = -\mathcal{J}^d(t)$, measures the action reward of battery discharge/charge to the demand charge at time slot t;
- $V^b(t) = -\mathcal{J}^b(t)$, measures the action reward of battery discharging to battery degradation at time slot t.

By setting the negative signs in front of $\mathcal{J}^e(t)$, $\mathcal{J}^d(t)$ and $\mathcal{J}^b(t)$, the function is expected to reward any action that leads the decrease of (1) energy charge, (2) demand charge, or (3) battery degradation.

Then, at the end of time slot t, the agent evaluates the performance of its action $a(t)$ using the defined reward function $R(t)$. During the following time slots, the agent aims to maximize the expected cumulative discounted reward: $\mathbb{E}[\sum_{t=1}^{\infty} \gamma^t R(t)]$, where $\gamma \in (0, 1]$ is a factor discounting future rewards.

Hence, the agent takes actions iteratively to approach the optimization objective as shown by Eq. (3.14a), through maximizing its reward step by step. As the time goes, this process is expected to converge to an optimized action (i.e., discharge/charge schedule) for operating the distributed BESS.

5.4.3 Learning Process Design

In traditional reinforcement learning, Q-table is applied for the learning process (namely Q-learning). Due to the limited dimension of state vectors that the Q-table can handle, deep Q-network (DQN) was proposed recently by combining the neural network with Q-learning algorithm and successfully applied for high dimension state learning problems. Thus, in this work we leverage the DQN to learn the optimal

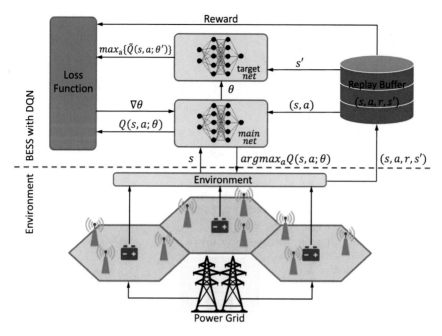

Fig. 5.3 The framework of BESS scheduling with DQN

BESS discharge/charge schedule. The proposed framework of BESS scheduling with DQN is illustrated in Fig. 5.3.

- **Replay Buffer**: The method of experience replay is adopted in DQN to eliminate the correlation among input data and improve the learning effectiveness. Specifically, every time interacting with the environment, the agent stores its experience reflecting the performance of its action into the replay buffer, in form of $\langle s(t), a(t), R(t), s(t+1)\rangle$. In the following iterations, the agent will randomly choose (a mini-batch of) the stored experience from the replay buffer and then the algorithm will update the neural network parameters (θ in Fig. 5.3) by means of stochastic gradient descent (SGD).
- **Neural Networks**: Two neural networks, main net and target net, are constructed in our framework. The parameters in the main net are updated in real-time in response to the environment, while the target net copies the parameters from the main net every κ time slots. For an arbitrary time slot t, after receiving environment states, the main net generates the Q-value by:

$$Q(s(t), a(t)) \leftarrow \mathbb{E}\big[R(t) + \gamma \cdot \mathbb{E}[Q(s(t+1), a(t+1))]\big] \tag{5.17}$$

where θ is the difference of network parameters between the main net and target net, and γ is the factor discounting the accumulative reward.

Algorithm 2: DQN training

Input: Power demands of BSs p_n, $1 \leq n \leq N$
Output: Discharge/charge actions $a(t)$, $1 \leq t \leq T$

1 Initialize replay buffer (RB) to capacity N;
2 Initialize main network Q with random weights θ;
3 Initialize target network $\tilde{Q}$ with weights $\tilde{\theta} = \theta$;
4 **for** $iteration = 1 : MaxLoop$ **do**
5   **for** $t = 1 : T$ **do**
6   Get environment state $s(t)$;
7        $a(t) = \begin{cases} \mathrm{argmax}_a Q(s(t), a(t); \theta), & \text{prob. } \epsilon \\ \text{random action}, & \text{prob. } 1 - \epsilon \end{cases}$
8   Execute action $a(t)$ and receive $R(t)$ and $s(t + 1)$;
9   Store $\langle (s(t), a(t), R(t), s(t + 1) \rangle$ into RB;
10   Randomly sample a mini-batch of experience $\langle s(i), a(i), R(t), s(i + 1) \rangle$ from RB;
11      $F(i) = \begin{cases} R(i), & \text{terminates at step } i + 1 \\ R(i) + \gamma \cdot \mathrm{max}_a \{\tilde{Q}(s, a; \tilde{\theta})\}, & \text{else} \end{cases}$
12   Perform SGD on $(F(i) - Q(s, a; \theta))^2$ w.r.t. θ;
13   Set $\tilde{Q} = Q$ by every κ steps;

- **Loss Function**: The main net updates its network parameters through the following loss function, by minimizing the mean squared error (MSE) between its Q-value and the Q-value of target net:

$$L(\theta) \leftarrow \mathbb{E}[(\tilde{Q} - Q(s, a; \theta))^2] \qquad (5.18)$$

where θ is the main net parameters, and $\tilde{Q}$ is the Q-value of target net and calculated by:

$$\tilde{Q} \leftarrow R + \gamma \cdot \mathrm{max}_a \{Q(s, a; \tilde{\theta})\} \qquad (5.19)$$

in which $\tilde{\theta}$ is the target net parameters and updates every κ time slots by copying those of the main net.

The DQN training process is depicted by the pseudo-code in Algorithm 2. First, the agent initializes the network parameters θ (Lines 1–3). Then, at each time slot t, the agent gets the environment state $s(t)$ and then selects an action $a(t)$ based on ϵ-greedy method (i.e., randomly selecting the action with the probability of $1 - \epsilon$), and chooses the action $\mathrm{argmax}_a Q(s(t), a(t); \theta)$ (Lines 6–7). After taking the action and interacting with the environment, the agent receives the reward $R(t)$ and observes the next state $s(t + 1)$ of the environment, and then stores the experience $\langle (s(t), a(t), R(t), s(t + 1) \rangle$ into replay buffer (RB) (Lines 8–9). After interacting with the environment by randomly choosing (a mini-batch of) stored experience, the agent updates the main network parameters with SGD (Lines 10–12). The target network copies the parameters of the main network every κ time slots (Line 13).

Essentially, our DRL-based approach introduced above is different from all previous work performing offline BESS scheduling with fixed/known power demands. To be detailed, after training with adequate historical power demands data from the BSs, the DQN can make real-time decisions on discharge/charge scheduling of the BESS in a distributed manner. The output action from the DQN at each time slot (i.e., $a(t)$) gives the detailed power discharging or charging amount for each battery in the network system. According to our experimental results, the training process usually gets converged in several hundred iterations (refer to the convergence analysis by Fig. 5.7 in Sect. 5.5.3).

5.5   Experimental Evaluations

5.5.1   Experiment Setup

5.5.1.1   BS and Traffic Demand Data

We consider a real-world BS deployment scenario in the downtown area of a metropolis in China. The locations of 2, 282 (4G/LTE) BSs are extracted from an open dataset on worldwide BS information [83], and we mark them on the map in Fig. 5.4. Based on the traffic load patterns of BSs from the mobile operators in this

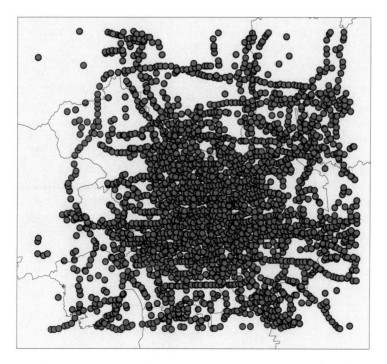

Fig. 5.4 The BS map of the downtown area of a metropolis in China. Each point shows the location of corresponding BS and the total number of BSs used in our experiments is 2282

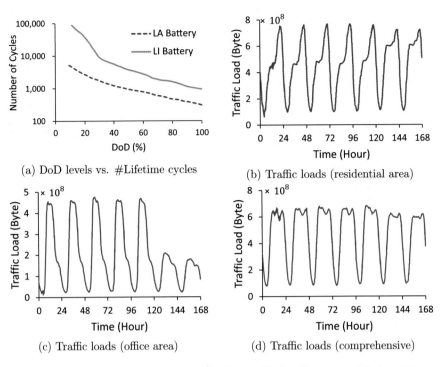

Fig. 5.5 (**a**) Relationship between DoD levels and battery lifetime (in number of discharge/charge cycles) for LA and LI batteries, respectively [86]. (**b**)–(**d**) Aggregated traffic loads of BSs at the residential, office and comprehensive areas, respectively, in one week period [67]

metropolis, all the BSs considered in this scenario could be divided into five types, mainly determined by the areas where they are located [67]. Particularly, the traffic demands from BSs at the areas of *resident, office*, and *comprehensive* account for nearly 90% of the total demands (resident: 17.55%, office: 45.72%, comprehensive: 24.81%). Thus, we only consider these three types of BSs in our experiments and their traffic demands within one-week period are illustrated in Fig. 5.5b–d, respectively. We then refer to the relationship between the traffic demand and power consumption given by Fig. 4.2b and derive the power demands of corresponding BSs, assuming that the 4G/LTE BSs will be upgraded to 5G ones in the future.

5.5.1.2 Parameter Settings

For the BESS battery types, we consider two mainstream batteries as BESS on the current market: lead-acid (LA) and lithium-ion (LI). We first follow the common practice at reserved time setting for backup battery provision [61], and the battery capacity at each BP is set to support the peak power demand from corresponding VC for up to 12 hours. We then refer to [73, 84, 85] for parameter settings of electricity

Table 5.1 Parameter settings

	Parameter	Setting
Billing policy	Billing cycle window $\mathcal{W}$	one month (30 days)
	Energy charge price λ_e[a]	$0.049/kWh
	Demand charge price λ_d[a]	$16.08/kW
	Battery cost λ_b[b]	$260/kWh(LA); $271/kWh(LI)
Battery config.	Discharge efficiency α	75% (LA); 85% (LI)
	Charge efficiency β	99.7% (LA); 99.9% (LI)
	Max charge rate $R+$	16 MW (LA); 16 MW (LI)
	Max discharge rate $R-$	8 MW (LA); 8 MW (LI)

[a] Prices of energy/demand charges in 2018, referring to the contract in [84]. Since we cannot find any public contract for energy/demand charges in China, the US prices are used only as a rough estimation
[b] Battery capacity costs in 2018, referring to the data in [85]

billing policy and BESS configurations. The parameter settings are summarized in Table 5.1.

5.5.1.3 Scenario Settings

We compare and analyze the overall energy cost (including energy charge, demand charge and batter cost), detailed scheduling results and return of investment (ROI) for the following scenarios:

- **All w/o BESS**: where all BSs are not equipped with BESS (the situation of current cellular networks);
- **All w/BESS**: where all BSs are equipped with BESS and operated by our DRL-based scheduling strategy;
- **Part w/BESS**: where only part (10, 30, and 50%) of the BSs are randomly chosen to equip with BESS and operated by the DRL-based scheduling approach.

5.5.2 General Performance at Cost Reduction with BESS

The results from all the set scenarios are summarized in Table 5.2, from which we have the following major findings.

5.5.2.1 All w/BESS

Compared with **All w/o BESS**, the cost reduction under this scenario is obvious. In one billing cycle (30 days), the overall cost savings are US$9,984 and US$15,405

Table 5.2 Results summary (one billing cycle)

	Energy charge ($)		Demand charge ($)		Battery cost ($)		Cost saving ($)		Saving ratio (%)	
	LA	LI	LA	LI	LA	LI	LA	LI	LA	LI
All w/o BESS	77,709	77,709	61,612	61,612	0	0	–	–	–	–
Part (10%)	77,825	77,780	60,067	59,940	400	39	1029	1562	0.74	1.12
Part (30%)	78,090	77,922	56,978	56,527	1060	109	3193	4763	2.29	3.42
Part (50%)	78,459	78,019	53,889	53,246	2020	181	4954	7874	3.56	5.65
All w/BESS	79,022	78,309	46,165	45,231	4151	376	9984	15,405	7.17	11.06

for the LA and LI battery cases, respectively, corresponding to saving ratios of 7.17% and 11.06%, respectively. The demand charges are cut down significantly by 25.07% and 26.59% with LA and LI, respectively. Meanwhile, the energy charge slightly increases due to the energy loss in discharging and recharging. Thanks to the improvement of energy storage technologies, the battery degradation cost keeps at a well accepted level.

5.5.2.2   Part w/BESS

The cost reduction grows with the increase of BESS deployment scale. For the LI battery case, the resulting cost saving ratios from 10, 30, and 50% BESS deployment scales are 1.12, 3.42, and 5.65%, respectively. The energy loss from discharge/charge cycles and battery degradation cost increase accordingly with the growth of BESS deployment scale.

With All w/BESS, therefore, the yearly cost saving of the mobile operators could reach up to US$120,000 and US$185,000 in the LA and LI battery cases, respectively, merely for the 2282 5G BSs in one city. Considering that the Telecom revenue growth is getting slower [63], such a cost reduction is a considerable saving for the mobile operators.

5.5.3   Case Studies of DRL-Based BESS Scheduling

To study details of the BESS scheduling solutions from our DRL-based approach, we look into the BESS discharge/charge results at three BSs with different power demand patterns, in a one-day scheduling period. The results are illustrated in Fig. 5.6.

5.5.3.1   From an Overall View

The DRL-based approach can learn and adapt to the general power demand patterns of the BSs during the whole time period. This can be verified by the reshaped power demand curves, showing that the BESS charges itself in off-peak power time slots and releases power in peak power time slots. Such a scheduling ability might be possessed by previous model-based approaches, in dealing with the global trend of (offline) power demands.

5.5.3.2   From Local Views

The DRL-based approach can capture the dynamic changes precisely. We can see that, when the power demand increases/decreases sharply in a very short time, the

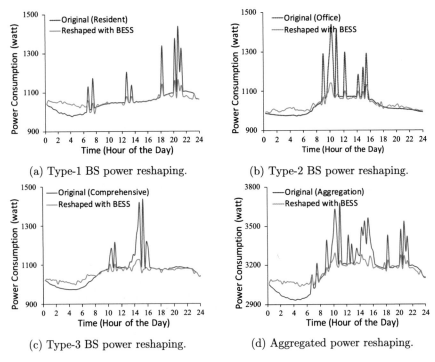

(a) Type-1 BS power reshaping.   (b) Type-2 BS power reshaping.

(c) Type-3 BS power reshaping.   (d) Aggregated power reshaping.

Fig. 5.6 (**a**) Relationship between DoD levels and battery lifetime (in number of discharge/charge cycles) for LA and LI batteries, respectively [86]. (**b**)–(**d**) Aggregated traffic loads of BSs at the residential, office and comprehensive areas, respectively, in one week period [67]

BESS can make prompt response with a proper discharging/charging operation. This capability of tackling dynamic and uncertain power demands makes our approach superior to others in real-time BESS scheduling.

In addition, the convergence of DQN training process with our DRL-based approach is illustrated in Fig. 5.7 (for one arbitrary BS case). With one-week historical power demands data, the DQN in our case can be well trained after about 300 iterations, taking less than one hour on a commodity computer. The trained DQN is then applied for BESS scheduling in real-time, typically taking seconds for one decision-making.

5.5.4   ROIs of Different BESS Deployments

The return of investment (ROI) is a financial metric defined by the benefit (cost saving in our case) divided by the total investment. It measures the probability of gaining a return from an investment and has been widely used to evaluate the efficiency of an investment [87]. With the capacity costs of batteries (given in

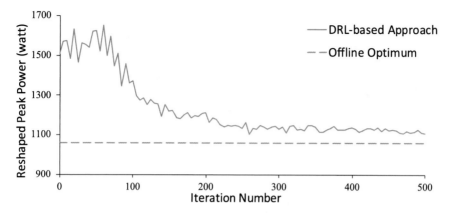

Fig. 5.7 Convergence of DQN training process

Table 5.3 ROIs of scenarios with LA and LI batteries, respectively

Scenario	ROI (LA BESS)	ROI (LI BESS)
Part (10%) w/BESS	4.31%	6.44%
Part (30%) w/BESS	4.42%	6.53%
Part (50%) w/BESS	4.47%	6.66%
All w/BESS	4.58%	6.81%

Table 5.1), the total investments under different scenarios can be calculated. With cost saving values in Table 5.2, the ROIs can thus be derived.

The ROIs for different scales of BESS deployment are shown in Table 5.3. We can find that with the LI battey, the ROI under scenario of **All w/ BESS** reaches 6.81%, indicating a relatively high investment efficiency. As the capacity cost of battery storage is estimated to decrease dramatically in the future (especially for the LI battery [88]), the ROI from large-scale BESS deployment could highly rise.

5.6 Related Work

In this section, we review relevant work on peak power demand shaving with battery energy storage system.

5.6.1 General System Peak Power Shaving with BESS

The optimal BESS discharge/charge scheduling problem was first investigated in [77], and a dynamic programming based approach was presented to tackle this problem for the general power system. A similar DP approach was applied in the later work of [78], in which the optimal sizing problem of BESS was also investigated. Although proved effective for the BESS operating in load reshaping and peak power shaving, the methods proposed are only applicable for one battery (as also presented in [89, 90]), which are different from the distributed batteries scenario in our case.

5.6.2 DC Peak Power Shaving with Centralized BESS

There are a great number of works leveraging the centralized BESS (i.e., the UPS) for data center (DC) peak power shaving. In [73], assuming that the power demands were all/partial known in a billing cycle, peak shaving methods with optimal DC battery control were presented to save the energy cost. Specifically, workload shifting strategies were leveraged in operating the battery, whereas in our problem, the workload (user traffic demands) cannot be shifted. The authors of [75] used energy storage in DC for peak demand charge reduction and regulation market participation jointly, and showed that the joint fashion with energy storage was superior than either separated one. The operating strategies in this work, however, were designed for one battery and based on known power demands, which are not suitable to our problem.

5.6.3 DC Peak Power Shaving with Distributed BESS

A distributed battery deployment scenario was considered for CDNs in [76], where a model for optimal battery provision was proposed to minimize the total power supply of distributed DCs. The battery discharge/charge scheduling, however, was not touched in this work. As the most relevant work to ours, [86] targeted a distributed battery scenario in the DC with fine-grained power backup at server level. It also purposed to reduce the peak power demand of the whole DC, whereas the BESS discharge/charge schedule was not optimized but chosen from pre-set policies, e.g., random discharging, least-recently-used (LRU) discharging and max-SoH discharging.

For peak power shaving of cellular networks in 5G and beyond, we are the first to (re)use the BS backup batteries as a distributed BESS system. The scale of batteries in our work is much larger than that in all previous work. Furthermore, the BESS operating schedule with our DRL-based approach is determined in a learning fashion, rather than those based on fixed models [76] or pre-set policies [86].

5.7 Conclusion

To cut down the energy cost of mobile operators in the shift to 5G and beyond, we proposed to reuse the backup batteries of BSs as a distributed BESS for peak demanded power shaving. An optimization problem to minimize the total energy cost was established, incorporating the BESS discharge/charge scheduling with practical considerations in electricity billing policy and battery specifications. To solve the problem under the dynamic power demands, we proposed a DRL-based approach that accommodates all factors in the modeling phase and makes decisions in real-time. Using real-world BS deployment and traffic demand data, the experiments under different scenarios show that our solution can significantly cut down the peak power demand charge and total energy cost for the mobile operators.

Chapter 6
Software-Defined Power Supply to Geo-Distributed Edge DCs

6.1 Introduction

With ever-increasing demands for computation, communication, and storage, the worldwide data centers (DCs) are scaling out and scaling up rapidly. Such a continuous expansion of DCs incurs enormous energy consumption and has drawn much attention in recent years. Since 2010, the energy consumption of global DCs grew at a compound annual growth rate (CAGR) of 4.4%; up to 2018, the energy consumption of DCs around the world reached 205 terawatt-hours, accounting for about 1% of global electricity consumption [91]. Among all the energy consumption, a considerable proportion comes from "brown energy" (i.e., the energy produced by fossil fuel), bringing enormous carbon footprints and significant environmental concerns.

Thanks to the continuous decline of material expense and installation cost for renewable energy generators (REGs) (e.g., a 61% cost reduction of the solar equipment from 2010 to 2017 [92]), renewable energy has been promoted dramatically over the past decade. Recently, *net-zero DC* entirely powered by renewable energy has been proposed [93]. It targets reducing the carbon emission (or equivalent) of a data center to zero or negative. Potential approaches in pursuing a near net-zero DC include (1) increasing the proportion of renewable energy supply [94, 95], (2) adopting efficient energy-saving methods [96–98], and improving the energy efficiency of ICT and non-ICT equipment [99, 100].

To achieve a complete net-zero DC, however, we are faced with three major challenges. **Firstly**, the supply of green energy (like solar or wind energy) is usually insufficient in the long term, compared to the large power demand of the data center. Then, how to improve the green energy supply efficiently is a crucial problem. **Secondly**, the generation of green energy is intermittent, unstable, and hard to predict in the short term, which makes the power supply misalign the power demand of data centers. The mismatch between the demand and supply increases the lack of green energy and leads to low utilization of renewable energy. **Thirdly**, while the battery energy storage system (BESS) is widely adopted in DCs and could help alleviate the mismatch, how to strategically operate the BESS (in terms of discharging/charging) and minimize the mismatch is a challenging problem.

As more and more edge DCs are going to be built along with the booming of edge computing services/applications [101], we in this chapter explore the potential of carbon emission reduction for *multiple* geo-distributed DCs at the network edge (namely *edge DCs*). To tackle the challenges mentioned above and pursue zero carbon emissions for the edge DCs, we design a software-defined power supply (SDPS) architecture to maximize the overall utilization of renewable energy. Specifically, to reduce the differences between power demand and supply, we firstly integrate different REGs and edge DCs as a green cell and match the overall power demand with the overall power supply in the cell. Then, we use BESS as an auxiliary method to fine-tune the power supply and make power demand and supply more consistent.

We summarize the contributions of this work as follows:

- To achieve net-zero edge DCs, we propose a software-defined power supply architecture, which integrates the REGs, edge DCs and BESS to minimize the temporal discrepancy between the power supply and demand. We devise two-phase operations for (1) supply-demand match between REGs and edge DCs across green cells and (2) battery discharging/charging schedule within a cell, respectively.
- We model the two phases under the proposed architecture as two mixed integer programming (MIP) problems and maximize the overall utilization of renewable energy. The optimization process also considers the dynamic characteristic of power demand and supply, transmission loss of energy, battery specifications, and physical constraints.
- We evaluate the performance of proposed architecture and approaches based on real-world traces. The experimental results show that the software-defined power supply architecture can significantly improve the renewable energy utilization among geo-distributed edge DCs.

The rest of the chapter is organized as follows. In Sect. 6.2, we propose the software-defined power supply architecture toward net-zero edge DCs. Section 6.3 elaborates the system model and problem formulation. Section 6.4 shows the results of the experiments. Section 6.5 concludes the chapter.

6.2 Architecture of Software-Defined Power Supply (SDPS)

This section introduces our motivation for software-defined power supply and then presents the architecture of software-defined power supply for geo-distributed edge DCs.

6.2.1 Motivation and Design Rationales

To increase the renewable energy utilization in data centers, edge DC operators widely adopt auxiliary REGs (e.g., the solar photovoltaic system or wind turbines). Nevertheless, as renewable energy generation at one REG is highly relevant to its geographic location (which determines the intensity of sunlight or wind), the power supply is hardly consistent with the power demand of edge DCs. Usually, we see the power demand of an edge DC goes through peak and valley periodically, which may not match or may be opposite to the power generation pattern of local REGs. For example, the solar energy output reaches its maximum at noon, while the power demand of edge DCs serving the residential area is usually low in the daytime (when most residents leave home). Therefore, the conventional one-to-one power supply mode (i.e., one REG supplies power to one edge DC) most likely induces either surplus or shortage in terms of renewable energy generation.

Since the real-time power generated by a single REG can hardly meet the power demand of one edge DC, the intuitive idea is to integrate multiple REGs and edge DCs to alleviate the imbalance between the power supply and demand. Based on such an idea, we propose a new multiple-to-multiple power supply mode (multiple REGs supply power to multiple edge DCs simultaneously) to maximize the utilization of renewable energy. The multiple-to-multiple power supply mode consists of two operational phases. In **Phase-I**, we construct green cells by integrating multiple REGs and edge DCs. Inside a green cell, integrated REGs cooperatively provide green energy for integrated edge DCs. This phase aims to find the optimal match between power supply and demand via strategically integrating REGs and edge DCs. With Phase-I, although the power demand and supply inside a green cell are more consistent in the long term, the short term's discrepancy between power supply and demand still exists. Thus, in **Phase-II**, we use BESS as an auxiliary way to reduce further the mismatch between the power demand and supply within the green cell. BESS manages the power supply by charging or discharging according to the real-time difference between the power demand and supply. The objective of this phase is to determine the optimal BESS charging/discharging control policy.

6.2.2 Architecture Design

As shown in Fig. 6.1, the software-defined power supply architecture for geo-distributed edge DCs mainly consists of three components or modules: Analyzer, Integrator, and Central Optimizer.

Analyzer aims to gather and process the demand and supply data based on the requests and environment information. It consists of four sub-modules: power monitor, workload monitor, power profile generator, and workload profile generator. At each time slot, the power monitor and workload monitor continuously gather the

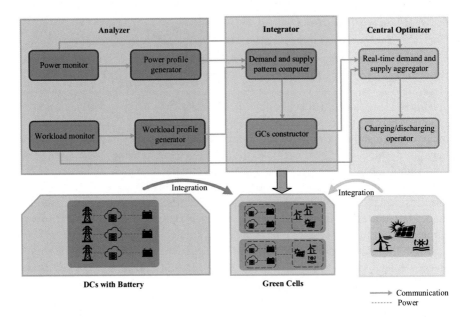

Fig. 6.1 Framework of software-defined power supply to edge DCs

real-time demand and supply data from REGs and edge DCs, respectively. The real-time data are used for the Central Optimizer to manage the battery operation at each time slot. The historical data about power and demand patterns are transmitted to the power profile generator and workload profile generator. Then the results are sent to the Integrator as critical inputs in constructing the green cells.

Integrator is the main module in forming the green cells. Based on the demand and supply patterns resulting from the Analyzer, it strategically selects edge DCs and REGs and groups them into different green cells (GCs). Inside each GC, multiple REGs jointly serve as the power supply and provide energy for multiple edge DCs. According to the historical data about each DC and REG in each GC, the *demand and supply pattern computer* finds the optimal matching policy to ensure that the demand can match the supply as much as possible (i.e., Phase-I optimization). Then, the GCs constructor builds up the green cells according to the matching policy received from the pattern computer. Note that the electrical cables among REGs and edge DCs can be pre-installed and reused along with existing ones. Thus the Integrator can reconstruct the GCs if a long-term change at the supply or demand side has been detected, e.g., when the edge DC's workload (so as the power demand) has changed. After forming or re-forming the GCs, the Integrator sends information about corresponding edge DCs and REGs in each GC to the Central Optimizer for further operations.

Central Optimizer controls the battery discharging/charging operations inside a green cell. Based on the information from Integrator and Analyzer, the Central Optimizer computes the optimal discharging/charging policy to maximize the utilization of renewable energy (i.e., Phase-II optimization). When the renewable energy exceeds the power demand, edge DCs are totally powered by REGs, and the Central Optimizer guides the battery to charge for extra energy storage. When the renewable energy is insufficient (less than the overall power demand), the Central Optimizer drives the battery to discharge to supply the edge DCs or uses the electricity grid if the stored energy is still insufficient.

Note that the Integrator and Central Optimizer are the key components of the software-defined power supply architecture: the former integrates both power supply and demand in a re-configurable way by considering the rough power mismatching from historical observations; the latter further regulates and fine-tunes the power mismatching to pursue zero-carbon emission. Conceptually, the re-configurable mechanism and fine-tuning operation in the above process make the power supply to edge DCs "software-defined."

6.3 Two-Phase Optimization in Software-Defined Power Supply

In this section, we present the system model and problem formulation for the two-phase optimization under the software-defined power supply architecture.

6.3.1 System Model

Without loss of generality, we target the scenario of geo-distributed edge DCs represented by a set of $\mathcal{N} = \{1, 2, \ldots, N\}$. Furthermore, we consider a discrete-time model, where the entire billing cycle (e.g., one month) is equally split into T consecutive slots with a length of Δt denoted by $\mathcal{T} = \{1, 2, \ldots, T\}$. An edge DC power demand is normally proportional to its volume of traffic load (like data analysis, image processing, etc.). In a certain period (e.g., one-week or one-month), the workload pattern of a commercial DC with a fixed customer group is usually stable and periodic, so is the corresponding power demand pattern. Thus, we denote the time-varying power demand of edge DC n at time slot t as $d_n(t)$. In addition, the location of the edge DC n is defined as l_n^{DC}, $n \in \mathcal{N}$, which is a vector representing the latitude and longitude of each DC.

In the above scenario of edge DCs, we introduce a set of geo-distributed REGs (the solar photovoltaic system or wind turbines), represented by $\mathcal{M} = \{1, 2, \ldots, M\}$. We denote the energy generation of REG m at time slot t as $s_m(t)$, and the location of all REGs as a vector of l_m^{REG}, $m \in \mathcal{M}$.

To fully use the renewable energy at the REGs, we further consider a battery energy storage system (BESS) attached to each edge DC (e.g., the backup batteries in the DC). We denote the battery capacity at edge DC n by π_n and the battery level (i.e., percentage of occupied energy capacity) at time slot t as $C_n(t)$. For simplicity, we discretize the battery level by $\{10, 20, \ldots, 100\%\}$ for discharging/charging operations.

6.3.2 Phase-I: Constructing Green Cells

Given the above system model, we depict the optimization problem of phase-I for constructing GCs. Specifically, multiple edge DCs and multiple REGs are included in a set of $\mathcal{K} = \{1, 2, \ldots, K\}$ GCs, where $K \leq \min(N, M)$. We use $X = (x_{m,k} \in \{0, 1\} : m \in \mathcal{M}, k \in \mathcal{K})$ to represent the connection between the REGs and the GCs, with $x_{m,k} = 1$ indicating that REG m belongs to GC k and $x_{m,k} = 0$ otherwise. Accordingly, we denote the connection relationship between the edge DCs and the GCs as $Y = (y_{n,k} \in \{0, 1\} : n \in \mathcal{N}, k \in \mathcal{K})$, where $y_{n,k} = 1$ indicates that edge DC n is connected with GC k.

Then, we can denote the integrated renewable energy generation of GC k in time slot t $S_k(t)$ as:

$$S_k(t) = \sum_{m=1}^{M} x_{m,k} s_m(t). \tag{6.1}$$

Accordingly, the integrated power demand of GC k in time slot t can be formulated as:

$$D_k(t) = \sum_{n=1}^{N} y_{n,k} d_n(t). \tag{6.2}$$

To improve the utilization of renewable energy, we aim to minimize the gap (or mismatching) between the power demand and supply in each green cell. For GC k, we define the gap between integrated renewable energy generation and power demand in time slot t as:

$$G_k(t) = (D_k(t) - S_k(t))^+, \tag{6.3}$$

where $(\cdot)^+$ means $\max(0, \cdot)$.

Given the above assumptions and conditions, we formulate the optimization problem as follows:

$$\underset{\{X,Y\}}{\text{Min}} \quad \sum_{k=1}^{K} \sum_{t=1}^{T} G_k(t), \tag{6.4}$$

$$s.t. \quad \sum_{k=1}^{K} x_{m,k} = 1, \quad \forall m \in \mathcal{M}, \tag{6.5}$$

$$\sum_{k=1}^{K} y_{n,k} = 1, \quad \forall n \in \mathcal{N}, \tag{6.6}$$

$$G_k(t) \leq \sum_{n=1}^{N} y_{n,k} \pi_n, \quad \forall k \in \mathcal{K}, \forall t \in \mathcal{T}, \tag{6.7}$$

$$x_{m,k} y_{n,k} ||l_m^{REG} - l_n^{DC}||_2 \leq L, \forall n \in \mathcal{N}, m \in \mathcal{M}, k \in \mathcal{K}. \tag{6.8}$$

The decision variables are X and Y, which explicitly show how the GCs are formed. Equations (6.5) and (6.6) indicate that all the REGs and edge DCs must belong to one GC. Equation (6.7) ensures that the gap between the supply and demand during the entire billing cycle cannot exceed the battery capacity in a GC. Considering the line loss in power transmission, we use Eq. (6.8) to constrain that the distance between the corresponding edge DCs and REGs in a GC is not beyond a certain range L.

6.3.3   Phase-II: BESS Discharging/Charging Operations

This phase further reduces the gap between renewable energy generation and power demand by leveraging the BESS discharging/charging operations. For the battery of edge DC n, we denote the discharging/charging operation at time slot t as $B_n(t)$, which reflects the amount of power discharging/charging. The positive $B_n(t)$ indicates discharging power from the battery to the edge DCs, and the negative indicates charging from renewable energy to the battery. Thus, the battery updates its level in each time slot following:

$$C_n(t) = C_n(t-1) - \frac{B_n(t) \cdot \Delta t}{\pi_n}. \tag{6.9}$$

For GC k, we define the gap between renewable energy generation and power demand after battery discharging/charging operations:

$$\tilde{G}_k = (D_k(t) - S_k(t) - \sum_{n=1}^{N} y_{n,k} B_n(t))^+. \tag{6.10}$$

Aiming at maximizing the utilization of renewable energy in each green cells, we formulate the optimization problem of phase-II as follows:

$$\operatorname*{Min}_{B_n} \sum_{k=1}^{K} \sum_{t=1}^{T} \tilde{G}_k(t), \tag{6.11}$$

$$\text{s.t.} \quad C_{min} \leq C_n(t) \leq C_{max}, \quad \forall n \in \mathcal{N}, t \in \mathcal{T}, \tag{6.12}$$

$$-R^+ \leq B_n(t) \leq R^-, \quad \forall n \in \mathcal{N}, t \in \mathcal{T}, \tag{6.13}$$

$$\frac{\sum_{t \in \tau} B_n(t) \cdot \Delta t}{\pi_n} \leq DoD_{max}, \forall n \in \mathcal{N}, \tau \in \Gamma. \tag{6.14}$$

In the above problem, the decision variables are B_n. Equation (6.12) prevents the battery from over-discharging/charging. C_{max} and C_{min} represent the upper and lower bounds of battery capacity, respectively. Equation (6.13) constrains the discharging/charging operations by the maximum charging rate and maximum discharging rate, denoted as R^+ and R^-, respectively. Since the continuous deep discharge is foul for the battery health, Eq. (6.14) limits the maximum depth of discharge, where Γ represents the set of the arbitrary continuous discharge time slots.

Since the power demand of edge DCs is dynamic and hard to predict accurately, it can only be obtained in real-time at every slot t. Thus, the above optimization problem cannot be solved directly. To avoid the problem, we transform the above optimization problem into an offline form at time slot $\tilde{t}$ as follows:

$$\operatorname*{Min}_{B_n(\tilde{t})} \sum_{k=1}^{K} \tilde{G}_k(\tilde{t}) + \delta \sum_{n=1}^{N} B_n(\tilde{t}), \tag{6.15}$$

$$\text{s.t.} \quad C_{min} \leq C_n(\tilde{t}) \leq C_{max}, \quad \forall n \in \mathcal{N}, \tag{6.16}$$

$$-R^+ \leq B_n(\tilde{t}) \leq R^-, \quad \forall n \in \mathcal{N}, \tag{6.17}$$

$$\frac{\sum_{t \in \tau} B_n(t) \cdot \Delta t}{\pi_n} \leq DoD_{max}, \forall n \in \mathcal{N}, \tau \in \tilde{\Gamma}, \tag{6.18}$$

where $\tilde{\Gamma}$ represents the set of the arbitrary continuous discharge time slots before $\tilde{t}$. In the offline optimization problem, we introduce an incentive parameter δ into the objective function. The added term $\delta \sum_{n=1}^{N} B_n(\tilde{t})$ stimulates the charging operations and $\delta \leq 1$ guarantees that the charging operations happen only when there is extra renewable energy after consumption. Then we can obtain the optimal solution by iteratively solving the optimization problem (6.15) at each time slot $\tilde{t}$.

6.4 Experimental Evaluations

In this section, we evaluate the performance of our solution using real-world trace data and compare the results with those from conventional solutions.

6.4.1 Experiments Setup

In a target area (e.g., powered by the micro-grid), we consider $N = 100$ edge DCs, which are supplied by $M = 100$ REGs as well as the traditional power grid. We generate the renewable energy patterns of REGs according to [102]. For the power demand of each DC, we derive the workload patterns from NORDUnet [103]. Generally, the energy consumption of edge DCs is directly proportional to the workload [104]. Thus, by assuming the configuration of edge DCs, we can roughly estimate the energy consumption. Accordingly, we denote the entire billing cycle T and time slot Δt as one day and 0.25 hours, respectively.

For comparison, we implement another two policies as the baselines in our experiments.

- **One-to-one**: It is the conventional policy that one edge DC is served by only one nearby REG. Such a mechanism usually has low utilization of renewable energy due to the mismatch between the supply and the demand.
- **GC-only**: It is the policy that multiple REGs and edge DCs are integrated into GCs without the BESS. The construction of GCs is of great help to alleviate the extra brown power consumption from the power grid.

6.4.2 Performance Comparison

We compare the performance of the proposed architecture with the above two baselines in a specific period. Figure 6.2 illustrates the total brown energy consumption of the system for three architectures during a day with different supply levels. Figure 6.2a–c correspond to the three different REGs supply levels, respectively. The high supply level corresponds to a clear day for solar panels and high wind intensity for wind turbines. The middle supply level corresponds to a partially cloudy day and moderate wind intensity. Similarly, the low supply level corresponds to a cloudy day and low wind intensity. Compared to the one-to-one policy, the GC-only policy significantly reduces the consumption of brown energy. It consumes 73.2, 67.5, and 54.6% less brown energy than the conventional one in three different cases, respectively.

By resorting to the charging/discharging operations of the BESS, SDPS further cuts down 100, 57.8, and 26.4% power consumption from the power grid in the three cases. From Fig. 6.2a, we can see that in the case of the high supply level,

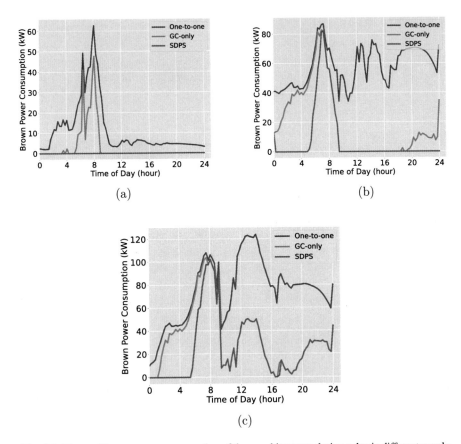

Fig. 6.2 The total brown power consumption of three architectures during a day in different supply levels. (**a**) High supply level. (**b**) Middle supply level. (**c**) Low supply level

SDPS reduces 100% brown power consumption compared to the conventional one-to-one architecture. When the renewable supply is sufficient, SDPS can use the extra power to achieve the net-zero edge DCs. In Fig. 6.2b, from 7 to 10 o'clock, the brown power consumption of GC-only and SDPS is almost the same. The SDPS does not work during the period due to the running out of stored power in BESS. No more energy is generated for charging, mainly because the low light intensity leads to the low output of solar panels. As shown in Fig. 6.2c, after 8 o'clock, BESS does not provide extra energy for edge DCs due to the low supply level, which means that batteries cannot gain supplement in time. Though BESS does not contribute much in this case, the integration of GCs still results in an excellent performance. Compared to the one-to-one architecture, SDPS consumes 66.6% less brown power.

6.5   Conclusion

We propose a software-defined power supply (SDPS) architecture for building net-zero edge data centers, which integrates multiple edge DCs and REGs to reduce brown energy consumption. Under the architecture, we formulate the two-phase operations as two optimization problems to minimize the power mismatching between demand and supply. Evaluation results demonstrate that the proposed SDPS architecture outperforms conventional one-to-one architecture concerning brown energy consumption at different supply levels. Also, the introduction of BESS in GCs is an efficient way to control the discrepancy of demand and supply patterns.

Chapter 7
Conclusions and Future Work

7.1 Conclusions

We looked into the energy dilemma faced by the mobile users, infrastructure/service providers in mobile edge computing. From some new perspectives, we provided the corresponding energy management and supply solutions in this book.

For the mobile users, we first investigated their low-battery anxiety by conducting a large-scale user survey. Specifically, we quantified the anxiety degree of mobile users and their likelihood of abandoning video watching with respect to the battery status, respectively. Leveraging the LBA model, we further developed a novel solution to low-power video streaming service at the network edge for mobile energy saving and LBA alleviating.

For the edge infrastructure and service operators, we first devised an optimal backup power deployment framework to cut down the backup battery cost in 5G networks. Then, we investigated the cost-saving potential of transforming the backup batteries to a distributed BESS in mobile networks. For geo-distributed edge DCs in the future edge computing environment, we proposed an integrated renewable energy supply architecture and a software-defined power supply mechanism to pursue zero-carbon emission.

7.2 Future Work

First, QoE measurement and enhancement are critical problems in mobile services. The LBA measurements and quantified LBA model in this work can be a powerful knob in the QoE-aware design and enhancement of mobile services/applications. Also, the neat methodology to model the LBA in this work could be also helpful in other scenarios. For example, it could be leveraged to quantify range anxi-

© The Author(s), under exclusive license to Springer Nature Singapore Pte Ltd. 2022   103
G. Tang et al., *GreenEdge: New Perspectives to Energy Management and Supply in Mobile Edge Computing*, SpringerBriefs in Computer Science,
https://doi.org/10.1007/978-981-16-9690-9_7

ety of battery electric vehicle (BEV) drivers [105], the result of which can be employed in driver emotion/behavior analysis and BEV charging infrastructure planning/deployment.

Second, the software-defined power supply architecture in pursing the net-zero edge DCs can also be applied in other distributed power systems, where the renewable energy generation and power demand are largely uncertain and heavily rely on the environment. In those cases, adaptive matching and BESS scheduling mechanisms could be studied to match power supply with demand. For example, a flexible power supply architecture with similar approaches has been exploited in base station systems of mobile networks [106].

Appendix A
Questionnaire of LBA Survey
and Collected Answers

In our survey, each of the participants was courteously requested to complete ten questions. Note that the original version of the questionnaire was in Chinese, as the voluntary participants are Chinese or comfortable with the language. We translate the questionnaire as follows for the purpose of information sharing. The information of i) the participants and their mobile phones, ii) the battery capacity status, and iii) the severity of LBA suffering are given in Tables A.1, A.2, and A.3, respectively.

1. Your gender:
○ Male
○ Female

2. Your age:
○ Under 18
○ 18~25
○ 35~45
○ 45~65
○ Above 65

3. Your occupation:
○ Student
○ Government/Institute
○ Company/Corporation
○ Freelancer
○ Others

© The Author(s), under exclusive license to Springer Nature Singapore Pte Ltd. 2022   105
G. Tang et al., *GreenEdge: New Perspectives to Energy Management and Supply in Mobile Edge Computing*, SpringerBriefs in Computer Science,
https://doi.org/10.1007/978-981-16-9690-9

4. Your mobile phone brand:

○ iPhone
○ Samsung
○ Huawei
○ Xiaomi
○ OPPO
○ Vivo
○ Others

5. Are you satisfied with the battery capacity of your mobile phone?

○ Satisfied
○ Just OK
○ Not satisfied

6. How many times do you have to charge your mobile phone daily (otherwise it would run out of power)?

○ ≤ 1
○ 2
○ 3
○ 4
○ >4

7. The frequency of your daily use of portable power bank (or backup battery):

○ Never use
○ Occasionally use
○ Frequently use

8. When inconvenient to charge the mobile phone, will you suffer from anxiety or panic when the battery level is low (say around 20%)?

○ Not at all
○ A little
○ Confirmed suffering
○ Severely suffering

9. At what battery level (in percentage from 0 to 100%) will you charge the mobile phone, when it is possible?

Empty   Full

0	20	40	60	80	100

You can drag the slider to select a value or enter the value directly in the left box.

10. At what battery level (in percentage from 1 to 100%) will you give up watching a video you are interested in, when you are browsing the *WeChat Moment* or *Weibo*?

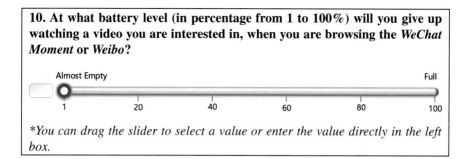

Almost Empty   Full

1   20   40   60   80   100

You can drag the slider to select a value or enter the value directly in the left box.

Table A.1 Participants and mobile phones: survey subjects and corresponding frequencies, $N = 2032$

Survey subjects	Frequency (%)
Meta info.	
# Cities	150
# Provinces[a]	31
# Countries	11
Gender (Q1)	
Male	1095 (53.89)
Female	937 (46.11)
Age (Q2)	
Under 18	9 (0.52)
18~25	888 (51.45)
25~35	460 (26.65)
35~45	250 (14.48)
45~65	119 (6.89)
Occupation (Q3)	
Student	1024 (50.39)
Gov/Inst	271 (13.34)
Company	434 (21.36)
Freelance	144 (7.09)
Others	159 (7.82)
Mobile phone share (Q4)	
iPhone	737 (36.27)
Huawei	682 (33.56)
Xiaomi	228 (11.22)
Others	385 (18.95)

[a] Provinces refer to provincial-level administrative units of China

Table A.2 Battery capacity
status: survey subjects and
corresponding frequencies,
$N = 2032$

Survey subjects	Frequency (%)
Battery satisfaction (Q5)	
Satisfied	819 (40.31)
Just OK	836 (41.14)
Not satisfied	377 (18.55)
Necessary charging frequency (Q6)	
≤ 1	764 (37.60)
2	1002 (49.31)
3	191 (9.40)
≥ 4	75 (3.69)
Portable charging frequency (Q7)	
Never use	400 (19.69)
Occasionally use	1423 (70.03)
Frequently use	209 (10.29)

Table A.3 Severity of LBA
suffering: survey subjects and
corresponding frequencies,
$N = 2032$

Survey subjects	Frequency (%)
Suffering of LBA and its severity (Q8)	
Not at all	165 (8.12)
A little	1173 (57.73)
Confirmed suffering	570 (28.05)
Severely suffering	124 (6.10)

Bibliography

1. STATISTA, "Number of smartphone users worldwide from 2016 to 2021(in billions)," https://www.statista.com/statistics/330695/number-of-smartphone-users-worldwide/, 2020.
2. X. Cao, G. Tang, D. Guo, Y. Li, and W. Zhang, "Edge federation: Towards an integrated service provisioning model," *IEEE/ACM Transactions on Networking*, vol. 28, no. 3, pp. 1116–1129, 2020.
3. HUAWEI, "5g telecom power target network (white paper)," https://carrier.huawei.com/~/media/CNBGV2/download/products/network-energy/5G-Telecom-Energy-Target-Network-White-Paper.pdf, 2019.
4. A. Carroll, G. Heiser *et al.*, "An analysis of power consumption in a smartphone." in *USENIX ATC*, vol. 14. Boston, MA, 2010, pp. 21–21.
5. G. Tang, K. Wu, Y. Wu, H. Liao, D. Guo, and Y. Wang, "Quantifying low-battery anxiety of mobile users and its impacts on video watching behavior," *arXiv preprint arXiv:2004.07662*, 2020.
6. MTN Consulting, "Operators facing power cost crunch," https://www.mtnconsulting.biz/product/operators-facing-power-cost-crunch/, 2020.
7. LG, "'Low battery anxiety' grips 9 out of ten people," https://www.lg.com/us/PDF/press-release/LG_Mobile_Low_Battery_Anxiety_Press_Release_FINAL_05_19_2016.pdf, May. 2016.
8. A. King, A. Valença, A. Silva, T. Baczynski, M. Carvalho, and A. Nardi, "Nomophobia: Dependency on virtual environments or social phobia?" *Computers in Human Behavior*, vol. 29, no. 1, pp. 140 – 144, 2013.
9. T. Taleb, K. Samdanis, B. Mada, H. Flinck, S. Dutta, and D. Sabella, "On multi-access edge computing: A survey of the emerging 5g network edge cloud architecture and orchestration," *IEEE Communications Surveys & Tutorials*, vol. 19, no. 3, pp. 1657–1681, 2017.
10. D. Kadjo, R. Ayoub, M. Kishinevsky, and P. V. Gratz, "A control-theoretic approach for energy efficient CPU-GPU subsystem in mobile platforms," in *Proceedings of DAC*. ACM, 2015, p. 62.
11. T. Zhang, X. Zhang, F. Liu, H. Leng, Q. Yu, and G. Liang, "etrain: Making wasted energy useful by utilizing heartbeats for mobile data transmissions," in *Proceedings of IEEE ICDCS*, 2015, pp. 113–122.
12. P. Stanley-Marbell, V. Estellers, and M. Rinard, "Crayon: saving power through shape and color approximation on next-generation displays," in *Proceedings of ACM EuroSys*, 2016, p. 11.

© The Author(s), under exclusive license to Springer Nature Singapore Pte Ltd. 2022
G. Tang et al., *GreenEdge: New Perspectives to Energy Management and Supply in Mobile Edge Computing*, SpringerBriefs in Computer Science, https://doi.org/10.1007/978-981-16-9690-9

13. Y. Chon, G. Lee, R. Ha, and H. Cha, "Crowdsensing-based smartphone use guide for battery life extension," in *UbiComp*. ACM, 2016, pp. 958–969.

14. A. J. Pyles, Z. Ren, G. Zhou, and X. Liu, "SiFi: exploiting VoIP silence for WiFi energy savings in smart phones," in *UbiComp*. ACM, 2011, pp. 325–334.

15. C. Min, C. Yoo, I. Hwang, S. Kang, Y. Lee, S. Lee, P. Park, C. Lee, S. Choi, and J. Song, "Sandra helps you learn: the more you walk, the more battery your phone drains," in *UbiComp*. ACM, 2015, pp. 421–432.

16. M. V. Heikkinen, J. K. Nurminen, T. Smura, and H. HäMmälnen, "Energy efficiency of mobile handsets: Measuring user attitudes and behavior," *Telematics and Informatics*, vol. 29, no. 4, pp. 387–399, 2012.

17. A. Rahmati, A. Qian, and L. Zhong, "Understanding human-battery interaction on mobile phones," in *MobileHCI*. ACM, 2007, pp. 265–272.

18. N. Banerjee, A. Rahmati, M. D. Corner, S. Rollins, and L. Zhong, "Users and batteries: interactions and adaptive energy management in mobile systems," in *Proceedings of ACM UbiComp*, 2007, pp. 217–234.

19. D. Ferreira, A. Dey, and V. Kostakos, "Understanding human-smartphone concerns - a study of battery life," in *PerCom*. IEEE, 2011, pp. 19–33.

20. Medium, "Who uses wechat and why is wechat so popular in China?" https://medium.com/@KaitlinZhang/who-uses-wechat-and-why-is-wechat-so-popular-in-china-c8df11577489, Oct. 2018.

21. M.-P. Tavolacci, G. Meyrignac, L. Richard, P. Dechelotte, and J. Ladner, "Problematic use of mobile phone and nomophobia among French college studentsmarie-pierre tavolacci," *European Journal of Public Health*, vol. 25, no. suppl_3, 2015.

22. X. Zhang, S. Sen, D. Kurniawan, H. Gunawi, and J. Jiang, "E2e: embracing user heterogeneity to improve quality of experience on the web," in *SIGCOMM*. ACM, 2019, pp. 289–302.

23. Hackernoon, "How much time do people spend on their mobile phones in 2017?" https://hackernoon.com/how-much-time-do-people-spend-on-their-mobile-phones-in-2017-e5f90a0b10a6, May. 2017.

24. Y. Liu, M. Xiao, M. Zhang, X. Li, M. Dong, Z. Ma, Z. Li, and S. Chen, "GoCAD: GPU-assisted online content-adaptive display power saving for mobile devices in internet streaming," in *Proceedings of WWW*. International World Wide Web Conferences Steering Committee, 2016, pp. 1329–1338.

25. A. Bhojan, "Adaptive video content manipulation for OLED display power management," in *Proceedings of ACM MobiQuitous*, 2018, pp. 236–245.

26. G. Tang, K. Wu, Y. Wu, H. Wang, and G. Qian, "Modelling and alleviating low-battery anxiety for mobile users in video streaming services," *IEEE Internet of Things Journal*, 2021.

27. W. Yuan and K. Nahrstedt, "Energy-efficient soft real-time CPU scheduling for mobile multimedia systems," in *ACM SIGOPS Operating Systems Review*, vol. 37, no. 5. ACM, 2003, pp. 149–163.

28. K. Lin, A. Kansal, D. Lymberopoulos, and F. Zhao, "Energy-accuracy trade-off for continuous mobile device location," in *Proceedings of ACM MobiSys*, 2010, pp. 285–298.

29. CNET, "Dell XPS 13 review: Drop the high-end display in dell's XPS 13 for better battery life," https://www.cnet.com/reviews/dell-xps-13-non-touch-2015-review/, 2019.

30. Y. C. Hu, M. Patel, D. Sabella, N. Sprecher, and V. Young, "Mobile edge computing—a key technology towards 5g," *ETSI white paper*, vol. 11, no. 11, pp. 1–16, 2015.

31. RTINGS.com, "OLED and LED tv power consumption and electricity cost," https://www.rtings.com/tv/learn/led-oled-power-consumption-and-electricity-cost, May. 2017.

32. M. Dong and L. Zhong, "Chameleon: a color-adaptive web browser for mobile OLED displays," in *Proceedings of ACM MobiSys*, 2011, pp. 85–98.

33. F. Liu, G. Tang, Y. Li, Z. Cai, X. Zhang, and T. Zhou, "A survey on edge computing systems and tools," *Proceedings of the IEEE*, vol. 107, no. 8, pp. 1537–1562, 2019.

34. NOKIA, "Airframe open edge server," https://www.nokia.com/networks/products/airframe-open-edge-server/, Jun. 2019.

35. Wowza Streaming Engine Transcoder Benchmarks, https://www.wowza.com/resources/Wowza_Transcoder_Benchmarks_Transrate720p.pdf, 2019.

36. 4D Systems, "Introduction to OLED displays design guide for active matrix OLED (amoled) displays," https://www.ruf.rice.edu/~mobile/elec518/readings/display/4D_AMOLED_Presentation.pdf, May. 2008.

37. L. Cheng, S. Mohapatra, M. El Zarki, N. Dutt, and N. Venkatasubramanian, "Quality-based backlight optimization for video playback on handheld devices," *Advances in Multimedia*, vol. 2007, 2007.

38. C.-H. Lin, P.-C. Hsiu, and C.-K. Hsieh, "Dynamic backlight scaling optimization: A cloud-based energy-saving service for mobile streaming applications," *IEEE Transactions on Computers*, vol. 63, no. 2, pp. 335–348, 2012.

39. N. Chang, I. Choi, and H. Shim, "DLS: dynamic backlight luminance scaling of liquid crystal display," *IEEE Transactions on Very Large Scale Integration Systems*, vol. 12, no. 8, pp. 837–846, 2004.

40. W.-C. Cheng and M. Pedram, "Power minimization in a backlit TFT-LCD display by concurrent brightness and contrast scaling," *IEEE Transactions on Consumer Electronics*, vol. 50, no. 1, pp. 25–32, 2004.

41. I. Choi, H. Shim, and N. Chang, "Low-power color TFT LCD display for hand-held embedded systems," in *Proceedings of ACM ISLPED*. ACM, 2002, pp. 112–117.

42. H.-Y. Lin, C.-C. Hung, P.-C. Hsiu, and T.-W. Kuo, "Duet: an oled & gpu co-management scheme for dynamic resolution adaptation," in *Proceedings of IEEE DAC*, 2018, pp. 1–6.

43. C.-H. Lin, C.-K. Kang, and P.-C. Hsiu, "Catch your attention: Quality-retaining power saving on mobile oled displays," in *Proceedings of IEEE DAC*, 2014, pp. 1–6.

44. Z. Yan and C. W. Chen, "Too many pixels to perceive: Subpixel shutoff for display energy reduction on oled smartphones," in *Proceedings of ACM MM*, 2017, pp. 717–725.

45. S. Pasricha, S. Mohapatra, M. Luthra, N. D. Dutt, and N. Venkatasubramanian, "Reducing backlight power consumption for streaming video applications on mobile handheld devices," in *ESTImedia*, 2003, pp. 11–17.

46. R. Yadav, W. Zhang, O. Kaiwartya, H. Song, and S. Yu, "Energy-latency tradeoff for dynamic computation offloading in vehicular fog computing," *IEEE Transactions on Vehicular Technology*, vol. 69, no. 12, pp. 14 198–14 211, 2020.

47. R. Yadav and W. Zhang, "Mereg: Managing energy-sla tradeoff for green mobile cloud computing," *Wireless Communications and Mobile Computing*, vol. 2017, 2017.

48. J. Ding, R. Cao, I. Saravanan, N. Morris, and C. Stewart, "Characterizing service level objectives for cloud services: Realities and myths," in *Proceedings of IEEE ICAS*, 2019, pp. 200–206.

49. A. Shye, B. Scholbrock, and G. Memik, "Into the wild: studying real user activity patterns to guide power optimizations for mobile architectures," in *Proceedings of IEEE/ACM MICRO*, 2009, pp. 168–178.

50. A. Shye, B. Scholbrock, G. Memik, and P. A. Dinda, "Characterizing and modeling user activity on smartphones: summary," in *Proceedings of ACM SIGMETRICS*. ACM, 2010, pp. 375–376.

51. G. Tang, H. Wang, K. Wu, and D. Guo, "Tapping the knowledge of dynamic traffic demands for optimal CDN design," *IEEE/ACM Transactions on Networking*, vol. 27, no. 1, pp. 98–111, 2018.

52. C. Ge, N. Wang, W. K. Chai, and H. Hellwagner, "QoE-assured 4K http live streaming via transient segment holding at mobile edge," *IEEE Journal on Selected Areas in Communications*, vol. 36, no. 8, pp. 1816–1830, 2018.

53. S. Wang, X. Zhang, Y. Zhang, L. Wang, J. Yang, and W. Wang, "A survey on mobile edge networks: Convergence of computing, caching and communications," *IEEE Access*, vol. 5, pp. 6757–6779, 2017.

54. PR Newswire, "Inspur releases OTII server for edge computing," https://www.prnewswire.com/news-releases/inspur-releases-otii-server-for-edge-computing-at-mwc-2019-300802977.html, Feb. 2019.

55. IBM CPLEX Optimizer, https://www.ibm.com/analytics/cplex-optimizer, 2020.

56. Gurobi Optimization, https://www.gurobi.com/, 2020.

57. CVX Research, http://cvxr.com/cvx/, 2019.

58. Twitch Statistics, https://twitchtracker.com/statistics, 2019.

59. G. Tang, Y. Wang, and H. Lu, "Shiftguard: Towards reliable 5g network by optimal backup power allocation," in *Proc. of IEEE SmartGridComm*, 2020, pp. 1–6.

60. M. Agiwal, A. Roy, and N. Saxena, "Next generation 5g wireless networks: A comprehensive survey," *IEEE Communications Surveys & Tutorials*, vol. 18, no. 3, pp. 1617–1655, 2016.

61. F. Wang, X. Fan, F. Wang, and J. Liu, "Backup battery analysis and allocation against power outage for cellular base stations," *IEEE Transactions on Mobile Computing*, vol. 18, no. 3, pp. 520–533, 2018.

62. G. Tang, D. Guo, K. Wu, F. Liu, and Y. Qin, "QoS guaranteed edge cloud resource provisioning for vehicle fleets," *IEEE Transactions on Vehicular Technology*, vol. 69, no. 6, pp. 5889–5900, 2020.

63. Statista, "Forecast growth worldwide telecom services spending from 2019 to 2023," https://www.statista.com/statistics/323006/worldwide-telecom-services-spending-growth-forecast/, 2020.

64. Argus Media, "5g rollout lifts lithium battery demand," https://www.argusmedia.com/en/news/2088490-chinese-5g-rollout-lifts-lithium-battery-demand, 2020.

65. F. Wang, F. Wang, X. Fan, and J. Liu, "BatAlloc: Effective battery allocation against power outage for cellular base stations," in *ACM e-Energy*, 2017, pp. 234–241.

66. X. Fan, F. Wang, and J. Liu, "On backup battery data in base stations of mobile networks: Measurement, analysis, and optimization," in *ACM CIKM*, 2016, pp. 1513–1522.

67. F. Xu, Y. Li, H. Wang, P. Zhang, and D. Jin, "Understanding mobile traffic patterns of large scale cellular towers in urban environment," *IEEE/ACM Transactions on Networking*, vol. 25, no. 2, pp. 1147–1161, 2016.

68. C. Zhang, H. Zhang, J. Qiao, D. Yuan, and M. Zhang, "Deep transfer learning for intelligent cellular traffic prediction based on cross-domain big data," *IEEE JSAC*, vol. 37, no. 6, pp. 1389–1401, 2019.

69. "Python pulp," https://pypi.org/project/PuLP/, 2020.

70. G. Tang, H. Yuan, D. Guo, K. Wu, and Y. Wang, "Reusing backup batteries as bess for power demand reshaping in 5g and beyond," in *Proc. of IEEE INFOCOM*, 2021.

71. J. Liu, M. Sheng, L. Liu, and J. Li, "Network densification in 5g: From the short-range communications perspective," *IEEE Communications Magazine*, vol. 55, no. 12, pp. 96–102, 2017.

72. H. Xu and B. Li, "Reducing electricity demand charge for data centers with partial execution," in *ACM e-Energy*, 2014, pp. 51–61.

73. M. Dabbagh, B. Hamdaoui, A. Rayes, and M. Guizani, "Shaving data center power demand peaks through energy storage and workload shifting control," *IEEE Transactions on Cloud Computing*, 2017.

74. H. Guo, J. Liu, J. Zhang, W. Sun, and N. Kato, "Mobile-edge computation offloading for ultradense IoT networks," *IEEE Internet of Things Journal*, vol. 5, no. 6, pp. 4977–4988, 2018.

75. Y. Shi, B. Xu, B. Zhang, and D. Wang, "Leveraging energy storage to optimize data center electricity cost in emerging power markets," in *ACM e-Energy*, 2016, pp. 1–13.

76. D. S. Palasamudram, R. K. Sitaraman, B. Urgaonkar, and R. Urgaonkar, "Using batteries to reduce the power costs of internet-scale distributed networks," in *ACM SoCC*, 2012, pp. 1–14.

77. D. K. Maly and K.-S. Kwan, "Optimal battery energy storage system (BESS) charge scheduling with dynamic programming," *IEE Proceedings-Science, Measurement and Technology*, vol. 142, no. 6, pp. 453–458, 1995.

78. A. Oudalov, R. Cherkaoui, and A. Beguin, "Sizing and optimal operation of battery energy storage system for peak shaving application," in *Lausanne Power Tech*. IEEE, 2007, pp. 621–625.

79. L. Chen, D. Yang, D. Zhang, C. Wang, J. Li *et al.*, "Deep mobile traffic forecast and complementary base station clustering for c-ran optimization," *Journal of Network and Computer Applications*, vol. 121, pp. 59–69, 2018.

80. Y. Guo and Y. Fang, "Electricity cost saving strategy in data centers by using energy storage," *IEEE Transactions on Parallel and Distributed Systems*, vol. 24, no. 6, pp. 1149–1160, 2012.

81. R. Urgaonkar, B. Urgaonkar, M. J. Neely, and A. Sivasubramaniam, "Optimal power cost management using stored energy in data centers," in *ACM SIGMETRICS*, 2011, pp. 221–232.

82. C.-K. Chau, G. Zhang, and M. Chen, "Cost minimizing online algorithms for energy storage management with worst-case guarantee," *IEEE Transactions on Smart Grid*, vol. 7, no. 6, pp. 2691–2702, 2016.

83. OpenCellid, https://opencellid.org/, 2020.

84. Dominion Energy South Carolina, Inc., "Rate 23 - industrial power service," https://etariff. psc.sc.gov/Organization/TariffDetail/150?OrgId=411, 2020.

85. US Department of Energy, "Energy storage technology and cost characterization report," https://www.energy.gov/eere/water/downloads/energy-storage-technology-and-cost-characterization-report, 2019.

86. B. Aksanli, T. Rosing, and E. Pettis, "Distributed battery control for peak power shaving in datacenters," in *IEEE IGCC*, 2013, pp. 1–8.

87. Wikipedia, "Return on investment," https://en.wikipedia.org/wiki/Return_on_investment, 2020.

88. National Renewable Energy Laboratory (NREL), "Cost projections for utility-scale battery storage," https://www.nrel.gov/docs/fy19osti/73222.pdf, 2019.

89. H. Wang and B. Zhang, "Energy storage arbitrage in real-time markets via reinforcement learning," in *IEEE Power & Energy Society General Meeting*, 2018, pp. 1–5.

90. L. Yang, M. H. Hajiesmaili, R. Sitaraman, A. Wierman, E. Mallada, and W. S. Wong, "Online linear optimization with inventory management constraints," *ACM POMACS*, vol. 4, no. 1, pp. 1–29, 2020.

91. E. Masanet, A. Shehabi, N. Lei, S. Smith, and J. Koomey, "Recalibrating global data center energy-use estimates," *Science*, vol. 367, no. 6481, pp. 984–986, 2020.

92. R. Fu, D. Feldman, R. Margolis, K. Ardani, and M. Woodhouse, "U.S. solar photovoltaic system cost benchmark: Q1 2017 report," in *EERE Publication and Product Library, Tech. Rep.*, 2017.

93. M. Arlitt, C. Bash, S. Blagodurov, Y. Chen, T. Christian, D. Gmach, C. Hyser, N. Kumari, Z. Liu, M. Marwah, A. McReynolds, C. Patel, A. Shah, Z. Wang, and R. Zhou, "Towards the design and operation of net-zero energy data centers," in *13th InterSociety Conference on Thermal and Thermomechanical Phenomena in Electronic Systems*, 2012, pp. 552–561.

94. Y. Li, A. Orgerie, and J. Menaud, "Opportunistic scheduling in clouds partially powered by green energy," in *IEEE International Conference on Data Science and Data Intensive Systems, DSDIS 2015, Sydney, Australia, December 11–13, 2015*. IEEE Computer Society, 2015, pp. 448–455.

95. T. Cioara, I. Anghel, M. Antal, S. Crisan, and I. Salomie, "Data center optimization methodology to maximize the usage of locally produced renewable energy," in *2015 Sustainable Internet and ICT for Sustainability, SustainIT 2015, Madrid, Spain, April 14–15, 2015*. IEEE Computer Society, 2015, pp. 1–8.

96. Q. Zhang, Q. Zhu, M. F. Zhani, and R. Boutaba, "Dynamic service placement in geographically distributed clouds," in *2012 IEEE 32nd International Conference on Distributed Computing Systems, Macau, China, June 18–21, 2012*. IEEE Computer Society, 2012, pp. 526–535.

97. H. Goudarzi and M. Pedram, "Geographical load balancing for online service applications in distributed datacenters," in *2013 IEEE Sixth International Conference on Cloud Computing, Santa Clara, CA, USA, June 28 - July 3, 2013*. IEEE Computer Society, 2013, pp. 351–358.

98. E. Jonardi, M. A. Oxley, S. Pasricha, A. A. Maciejewski, and H. J. Siegel, "Energy cost optimization for geographically distributed heterogeneous data centers," in *Sixth International Green and Sustainable Computing Conference, IGSC 2015, Las Vegas, NV, USA, December 14–16, 2015*. IEEE Computer Society, 2015, pp. 1–6.

99. L. Ganesh, H. Weatherspoon, T. Marian, and K. Birman, "Integrated approach to data center power management," *IEEE Trans. Computers*, vol. 62, no. 6, pp. 1086–1096, 2013.

100. E. Frachtenberg, A. Heydari, H. Li, A. Michael, J. Na, A. Nisbet, and P. Sarti, "High-efficiency server design," in *Conference on High Performance Computing Networking, Storage and Analysis, SC 2011, Seattle, WA, USA, November 12–18, 2011*, S. A. Lathrop, J. Costa, and W. Kramer, Eds. ACM, 2011, pp. 27:1–27:27.

101. L. Tong, Y. Li, and W. Gao, "A hierarchical edge cloud architecture for mobile computing," in *35th Annual IEEE International Conference on Computer Communications, INFOCOM 2016, San Francisco, CA, USA, April 10–14*, 2016. IEEE, 2016, pp. 1–9.

102. M. Raza, M. Nadarajah, and C. Ekanayake, "On recent advances in PV output power forecast," *Solar Energy*, vol. 136, pp. 125–144, 2016.

103. NORDUnet, http://stats.nordu.net/connections.html.

104. C. Wang, B. Urgaonkar, Q. Wang, G. Kesidi s, and A. Sivasubramaniam, "Data center power cost optimization via workload modulation," in *IEEE/ACM 6th International Conference on Utility and Cloud Computing, UCC 2013, Dresden, Germany, December 9–12, 2013*. IEEE Computer Society, 2013, pp. 260–263.

105. N. Rauh, T. Franke, and J. F. Krems, "Understanding the impact of electric vehicle driving experience on range anxiety," *Human factors*, vol. 57, no. 1, pp. 177–187, 2015.

106. H. Yuan, G. Tang, T. Liang, D. Guo, and Y. Wang, "Towards net-zero base stations with integrated and flexible power supply in future networks," *Accepted by IEEE Network Magazine*, 2021.

Printed in the United States
by Baker & Taylor Publisher Services